VENTURE CAPITAL DIRECTORY

Managing Partner David Anthony
21 Ventures, LLC
14 East 44th Street
3rd Floor
New York, New York 10017
212-699-0842
david@21ventures.net

Chairman and CEO Morton Meyerson
2M Technology Ventures, L.P.
3401 Armstrong Avenue
Suite 400
Dallas, Texas 75205-3949
214-443-1900
morton.meyerson@2m.com

Partner Robin Murray
3i Corporation
275 Middlefield Road
Menlo Park, California 94025
650-470-3200
robin.murray@3i.com

Managing Director Ronan Reid
4th Level Ventures
The Tower, Trinity College Enterprise Centre
Pearse Street
Dublin IE-2
Ireland
353-1-671-1288
ronan.reid@4thlevelventures.ie

Founder Ray Naughton
4th Level Ventures
The Tower, Trinity College Enterprise Centre
Pearse Street
Dublin IE-2
Ireland
353-1-671-1288
ray.naughton@4thlevelventures.ie

Managing Partner Johan Bjurström
ABN AMRO Capital
Birger Jarlsgatan 12
PO Box 26124
SE-10041 Stockholm

VENTURE CAPITAL DIRECTORY

Sweden
46-8-407-4440
johan.bjurstrom@abnamrocapital.com

Investment Director Johan Conradsson
ABN AMRO Capital
Birger Jarlsgatan 12
PO Box 26124
SE-10041 Stockholm
Sweden
46-8-407-4440
johan.conradsson@abnamrocapital.com

Investment Director Kristofer Runnquist
ABN AMRO Capital
Birger Jarlsgatan 12
PO Box 26124
SE-10041 Stockholm
Sweden
46-8-407-4440
kristofer.runnquist@abnamrocapital.com

Investment Director Johan Rydmark
ABN AMRO Capital
Birger Jarlsgatan 12
PO Box 26124
SE-10041 Stockholm
Sweden
46-8-407-4440
johan.rydmark@abnamrocapital.com

Partner Tommy Wikstrom
ABN AMRO Capital
Birger Jarlsgatan 12
PO Box 26124
SE-10041 Stockholm
Sweden
46-8-407-4440
tommy.wikstrom@abnamrocapital.com

Partner Patrick Bulmer
ABN AMRO Capital Ltd.
1 Carey Lane
London
EC2V 8AE
United Kingdom

VENTURE CAPITAL DIRECTORY

44-20-7678-8000
patrick.bulmer@uk.abnamro.com

Partner Dominic Collier
ABN AMRO Capital Ltd.
1 Carey Lane
London
EC2V 8AE
United Kingdom
44-20-7678-8000
dominic.collier@uk.abnamro.com

Partner Jonathan Bourn
ABN AMRO Capital Ltd.
1 Carey Lane
London
EC2V 8AE
United Kingdom
44-20-7678-8000
jonathan.bourn@uk.abnamro.com

Partner Andrew Moye
ABN AMRO Capital Ltd.
1 Carey Lane
London
EC2V 8AE
United Kingdom
44-20-7678-8000
andrew.moye@uk.abnamro.com

Partner Paul Moxon
ABN AMRO Capital Ltd.
1 Carey Lane
London
EC2V 8AE
United Kingdom
44-20-7678-8000
paul.moxon@uk.abnamro.com

Managing Partner Paul Southwell
ABN AMRO Capital Ltd.
1 Carey Lane
London
EC2V 8AE
United Kingdom
44-20-7678-8000

VENTURE CAPITAL DIRECTORY

paul.southwell@abnamrocapital.com

Partner Simon Tuttle
ABN AMRO Capital Ltd.
1 Carey Lane
London
EC2V 8AE
United Kingdom
44-20-7678-8000
simon.tuttle@uk.abnamro.com

Investment Manager Grant Paul Florence
ABN AMRO Capital Ltd.
1 Carey Lane
London
EC2V 8AE
United Kingdom
44-20-7678-8000

CEO Antonio Corbani
ABN AMRO Capital SpA
corso Magenta 10
IT-20123 Milan
Italy
39-2-802-91-81
antonio.corbani@abnamrocapital.com

Chairman Andrew Banks
ABRY Partners LLC
111 Huntington Avenue
Boston, Massachusetts 2199
617-859-2959
President Royce Yudkoff
ABRY Partners LLC
111 Huntington Avenue
Boston, Massachusetts 2199
617-859-2959
ry@abry.com

Managing Partner Peggy Koenig
ABRY Partners LLC
111 Huntington Avenue
Boston, Massachusetts 2199
617-859-2959
pkoenig@abry.com

VENTURE CAPITAL DIRECTORY

Managing Partner Jay Grossman
ABRY Partners LLC
111 Huntington Avenue
Boston, Massachusetts 2199
617-859-2959
jgrossman@abry.com

Partner Peni Garber
ABRY Partners LLC
111 Huntington Avenue
Boston, Massachusetts 2199
617-859-2959
pgarber@abry.com

Partner John Hunt
ABRY Partners LLC
111 Huntington Avenue
Boston, Massachusetts 2199
617-859-2959
dbudde@abry.com

Partner Erik Brooks
ABRY Partners LLC
111 Huntington Avenue
Boston, Massachusetts 2199
617-859-2959
ebrooks@abry.com

Partner Robert MacInnis
ABRY Partners LLC
111 Huntington Avenue
Boston, Massachusetts 2199
617-859-2959
rmacInnis@abry.com

Principal C.J. Brucato
ABRY Partners LLC
111 Huntington Avenue
Boston, Massachusetts 2199
617-859-2959
cbrucato@abry.com

Principal Roger Marrero
ABRY Partners LLC
111 Huntington Avenue
Boston, Massachusetts 2199

VENTURE CAPITAL DIRECTORY

617-859-2959
rmarrero@abry.com

Principal Blake Battaglia
ABRY Partners LLC
111 Huntington Avenue
Boston, Massachusetts 2199
617-859-2959
bbattaglia@abry.com

Principal Hilary Kaiser
ABRY Partners LLC
111 Huntington Avenue
Boston, Massachusetts 2199
617-859-2959
hkaiser@abry.com

Vice President Brent Stone
ABRY Partners LLC
111 Huntington Avenue
Boston, Massachusetts 2199
617-859-2959
bstone@abry.com

Vice President Brian St. Jean
ABRY Partners LLC
111 Huntington Avenue
Boston, Massachusetts 2199
617-859-2959
bstjean@abry.com

Vice President Azra Nanji
ABRY Partners LLC
111 Huntington Avenue
Boston, Massachusetts 2199
617-859-2959
ananji@abry.com

Chairman and Founding Partner Don Hebb
ABS Capital Partners
400 East Pratt Street
Suite 910
Baltimore, Maryland 21202-3116
410-246-5600
dhebb@abscapital.com

VENTURE CAPITAL DIRECTORY

General Partner Deric Emry
ABS Capital Partners
400 East Pratt Street
Suite 910
Baltimore, Maryland 21202-3116
410-246-5600
demry@abscapital.com

Founding Partner Tim Weglicki
ABS Capital Partners
400 East Pratt Street
Suite 910
Baltimore, Maryland 21202-3116
410-246-5600
tweglicki@abscapital.com

Managing General Partner John Stobo
ABS Capital Partners
1700 Montgomery Street
Suite 440
San Francisco, California 94111-1021
415-989-5100
jstobo@abscapital.com

General Partner Laura Witt
ABS Capital Partners
400 East Pratt Street
Suite 910
Baltimore, Maryland 21202-3116
410-246-5600
lwitt@abscapital.com

General Partner Bobby Goswami
ABS Capital Partners
1700 Montgomery Street
Suite 440
San Francisco, California 94111-1021
415-989-5100
bgoswami@abscapital.com

Managing General Partner Phil Clough
ABS Capital Partners
400 East Pratt Street
Suite 910
Baltimore, Maryland 21202-3116
410-246-5600

VENTURE CAPITAL DIRECTORY

pclough@abscapital.com

General Partner Ralph Terkowitz
ABS Capital Partners
400 East Pratt Street
Suite 910
Baltimore, Maryland 21202-3116
410-246-5600
rterkowitz@abscapital.com

General Partner Mark Anderson
ABS Capital Partners
400 East Pratt Street
Suite 910
Baltimore, Maryland 21202-3116
410-246-5600
manderson@abscapital.com

Principal Cal Wheaton
ABS Capital Partners
400 East Pratt Street
Suite 910
Baltimore, Maryland 21202-3116
410-246-5600
cwheaton@abscapital.com

CFO James Stevenson
ABS Capital Partners
400 East Pratt Street
Suite 910
Baltimore, Maryland 21202-3116
410-246-5600
jstevenson@abscapital.com

Principal Christopher Ackerley
Ackerley Partners, LLC
601 Union Street
Suite 3003
Seattle, Washington 98101
206-624-2888

Principal Ted Ackerley
Ackerley Partners, LLC
601 Union Street
Suite 3003
Seattle, Washington 98101

VENTURE CAPITAL DIRECTORY

206-624-2888

Principal Kim Ackerley Cleworth
Ackerley Partners, LLC
601 Union Street
Suite 3003
Seattle, Washington 98101
206-624-2888

CFO Kevin Hylton
Ackerley Partners, LLC
601 Union Street
Suite 3003
Seattle, Washington 98101
206-624-2888

CEO Cliff Girard
Acorn Ventures, Inc.
268 Bush Street
Suite 2829
San Francisco, California 94014
650-994-7801

Executive Vice President Charles Duff
Acorn Ventures, Inc.
268 Bush Street
Suite 2829
San Francisco, California 94014
650-994-7801
cduff@acorn-ventures.com

Partner Alun Branigan
Actis Capital Partners
55 Market Street #11-02
 48941
Singapore
65-6227-8632
abranigan@act.is

Investment Principal Kee Teng Koh
Actis Capital Partners
55 Market Street #11-02
 48941
Singapore
65-6227-8632

VENTURE CAPITAL DIRECTORY

Investment Principal Bharat Rao
Actis Capital Partners
55 Market Street #11-02
 48941
Singapore
65-6227-8632

President and CEO Ben Neumann
Ad-Ventures, LLC
11288 Ventura Blvd. #443 B
Studio City, California 91604
323-993-8664
brn@ad-ventures.com

President Steven Stull
Advantage Capital Partners
909 Poydras Street
Suite 2230
New Orleans, Louisiana 70112
504-522-4850
sstull@advantagecap.com

Senior Managing Director Scott Zajac
Advantage Capital Partners
909 Poydras Street
Suite 2230
New Orleans, Louisiana 70112
504-522-4850
szajac@advantagecap.com

Managing Director Crichton Brown
Advantage Capital Partners
909 Poydras Street
Suite 2230
New Orleans, Louisiana 70112
504-522-4850
cbrown@advantagecap.com

Managing Director Timothy Cockshutt
Advantage Capital Partners
16750 Gulf Blvd., No. 416
St. Petersburg, Florida 33708
727-319-6649
tcockshutt@advantagecap.com

Managing Director Maurice Doyle

VENTURE CAPITAL DIRECTORY

Advantage Capital Partners
909 Poydras Street
Suite 2230
New Orleans, Louisiana 70112
504-522-4850
mdoyle@advantagecap.com

Managing Director Michael Johnson
Advantage Capital Partners
909 Poydras Street
Suite 2230
New Orleans, Louisiana 70112
504-522-4850
mjohnson@advantagecap.com

Managing Director Scott Murphy
Advantage Capital Partners
5 Warren Street
Suite 204
Glens Falls, New York 12801
518-743-0060
smurphy@advantagecap.com

Managing Director Damon Rawie
Advantage Capital Partners
7733 Forsyth Boulevard
Suite 1850
St. Louis, Missouri 63105
314-725-0800
drawie@advantagecap.com

Senior Vice President Carter Dunkin
Advantage Capital Partners
7733 Forsyth Boulevard
Suite 1850
St. Louis, Missouri 63105
314-725-0800
cdunkin@advantagecap.com

Senior Vice President Tate Garrett
Advantage Capital Partners
16750 Gulf Blvd., No. 416
St. Petersburg, Florida 33708
727-319-6649
tgarrett@advantagecap.com

VENTURE CAPITAL DIRECTORY

Principal Ryan Brennan
Advantage Capital Partners
7733 Forsyth Boulevard
Suite 1850
St. Louis, Missouri 63105
314-725-0800
rbrennan@advantagecap.com

Principal Mark Lewis
Advantage Capital Partners
7733 Forsyth Boulevard
Suite 1850
St. Louis, Missouri 63105
314-725-0800
mlewis@advantagecap.com

Managing Director Kevin Caley
Advantage Early Growth Fund
PO Box 11679
Tamworth
B78 2YD
United Kingdom
44-121-311-0378
kevin@aegf.co.uk

Operations Director Peter Brown
Advantage Early Growth Fund
PO Box 11679
Tamworth
B78 2YD
United Kingdom
44-121-311-0378
peter@aegf.co.uk

Investment Manager Tim Powell
Advantage Early Growth Fund
PO Box 11679
Tamworth
B78 2YD
United Kingdom
44-121-311-0378
tim@aegf.co.uk

Operating Partner M. Eduardo Campiani
Advent International Corporation
Av. del Libertador 498 Floor 13 N

VENTURE CAPITAL DIRECTORY

Buenos Aires C1001ABR
Argentina
54-11-5077-8900
ecampiani@adventinternational.com

Partner Juan Pablo Zucchini
Advent International Corporation
Av. del Libertador 498 Floor 13 N
Buenos Aires C1001ABR
Argentina
54-11-5077-8900
jzucchini@adventinternational.com

Principal Nicolas Sujoy
Advent International Corporation
Av. del Libertador 498 Floor 13 N
Buenos Aires C1001ABR
Argentina
54-11-5077-8900
nsujoy@adventinternational.com

Associate Joaquín Mandachain
Advent International Corporation
Av. del Libertador 498 Floor 13 N
Buenos Aires C1001ABR
Argentina
54-11-5077-8900
jmandachain@adventinternational.com

Chief Executive, Latin America Ernest Bachrach
Advent International Corporation
Av. del Libertador 498 Floor 13 N
Buenos Aires C1001ABR
Argentina
54-11-5077-8900
ebachrach@adventinternational.com

Analyst Gabriel Kurman
Advent International Corporation
Av. del Libertador 498 Floor 13 N
Buenos Aires C1001ABR
Argentina
54-11-5077-8900
gkurman@adventinternational.com

Managing Director Juan Carlos Torres

VENTURE CAPITAL DIRECTORY

Advent International Corporation
Edificio Omega
Campos Eliseos 345 - 7 piso
Col. Polanco 11560
Mexico
52-55-5281-0303
jtorres@adventinternational.com

Partner Alfredo Alfaro
Advent International Corporation
Edificio Omega
Campos Eliseos 345 - 7 piso
Col. Polanco 11560
Mexico
52-55-5281-0303
aalfaro@adventinternational.com

Partner Diego Serebrisky
Advent International Corporation
Edificio Omega
Campos Eliseos 345 - 7 piso
Col. Polanco 11560
Mexico
52-55-5281-0303
dserebrisky@adventinternational.com

Principal Luis Solorzano
Advent International Corporation
Edificio Omega
Campos Eliseos 345 - 7 piso
Col. Polanco 11560
Mexico
52-55-5281-0303
lsolorzano@adventinternational.com

Principal Santiago Castillo
Advent International Corporation
Edificio Omega
Campos Eliseos 345 - 7 piso
Col. Polanco 11560
Mexico
52-55-5281-0303
scastillo@adventinternational.com

Analyst Rosendo Sáinz-Trápaga
Advent International Corporation

VENTURE CAPITAL DIRECTORY

Edificio Omega
Campos Eliseos 345 - 7 piso
Col. Polanco 11560
Mexico
52-55-5281-0303
rsainz@adventinternational.com

Analyst Guillermo Carmona
Advent International Corporation
Edificio Omega
Campos Eliseos 345 - 7 piso
Col. Polanco 11560
Mexico
52-55-5281-0303
gcarmona@adventinternational.com

Principal Antonio Moya-Angeler
Advent International Corporation
Edificio Omega
Campos Eliseos 345 - 7 piso
Col. Polanco 11560
Mexico
52-55-5281-0303
amoya@adventinternational.com

Chairman Peter Brooke
Advent International Corporation
75 State Street
Boston, Massachusetts 2109
617-951-9400
pbrooke@adventinternational.com

Managing Director and CFO Tom Lauer
Advent International Corporation
75 State Street
Boston, Massachusetts 2109
617-951-9400
tlauer@adventinternational.com

Managing Director David Mussafer
Advent International Corporation
75 State Street
Boston, Massachusetts 2109
617-951-9400
dmm@adventinternational.com

VENTURE CAPITAL DIRECTORY

Partner David McKenna
Advent International Corporation
75 State Street
Boston, Massachusetts 2109
617-951-9400
dmckenna@adventinternational.com

Partner Chris Pike
Advent International Corporation
75 State Street
Boston, Massachusetts 2109
617-951-9400
cpike@adventinternational.com

Partner Beverly Berman
Advent International Corporation
75 State Street
Boston, Massachusetts 2109
617-951-9400
bberman@adventinternational.com

Managing Director Bob Taylor
Advent International Corporation
75 State Street
Boston, Massachusetts 2109
617-951-9400
rtaylor@adventinternational.com

Partner Steven Collins
Advent International Corporation
75 State Street
Boston, Massachusetts 2109
617-951-9400
scollins@adventinternational.com

Partner and Treasurer Janet Hennessy
Advent International Corporation
75 State Street
Boston, Massachusetts 2109
617-951-9400
jhennessy@adventinternational.com

Principal Jeff Case
Advent International Corporation
75 State Street
Boston, Massachusetts 2109

VENTURE CAPITAL DIRECTORY

617-951-9400
jcase@adventinternational.com

Principal Chris Egan
Advent International Corporation
75 State Street
Boston, Massachusetts 2109
617-951-9400
cegan@adventinternational.com

Principal Gabriel Gomez
Advent International Corporation
75 State Street
Boston, Massachusetts 2109
617-951-9400
ggomez@adventinternational.com

Principal Stephen Hoffmeister
Advent International Corporation
75 State Street
Boston, Massachusetts 2109
617-951-9400
shoffmeister@adventinternational.com

Principal John Maldonado
Advent International Corporation
75 State Street
Boston, Massachusetts 2109
617-951-9400
jmaldonado@adventinternational.com

Advent International Ltda.
Partner Patrice N.B. Etlin
Rua Campos Bicudo, 98 - Conj. 52
São Paulo São Paulo
Brazil
04536-010
55-11-3371-3770
petlin@adventinternational.com

Advent International Ltda.
Operating Partner Erwin-Theodor Russel
Rua Campos Bicudo, 98 - Conj. 52
São Paulo São Paulo
Brazil
04536-010

VENTURE CAPITAL DIRECTORY

55-11-3371-3770
erussel@adventinternational.com

Advent International Ltda.
Principal Luiz Antonio Alves
Rua Campos Bicudo, 98 - Conj. 52
São Paulo São Paulo
Brazil
04536-010
55-11-3371-3770
lalves@adventinternational.com

Advent International Ltda.
Senior Associate Frederico Brito e Abreu
Rua Campos Bicudo, 98 - Conj. 52
São Paulo São Paulo
Brazil
04536-010
55-11-3371-3770
fabreu@adventinternational.com

Advent International Ltda.
Associate Mario Malta
Rua Campos Bicudo, 98 - Conj. 52
São Paulo São Paulo
Brazil
04536-010
55-11-3371-3770
mmalta@adventinternational.com

Advent International Ltda.
Analyst Jorge Maluf
Rua Campos Bicudo, 98 - Conj. 52
São Paulo São Paulo
Brazil
04536-010
55-11-3371-3770
jmaluf@adventinternational.com

Chairman John Walker
Advent International plc
111 Buckingham Palace Road
London
SW1W 0SR
United Kingdom
44-20-7333-0800

VENTURE CAPITAL DIRECTORY

jwalker@uk.adventinternational.com

Managing Director Will Schmidt
Advent International plc
111 Buckingham Palace Road
London
SW1W 0SR
United Kingdom
44-20-7333-0800
wschmidt@uk.adventinternational.com

Managing Director John Singer
Advent International plc
111 Buckingham Palace Road
London
SW1W 0SR
United Kingdom
44-20-7333-0800
jsinger@uk.adventinternational.com

Managing Director Steve Tadler
Advent International plc
111 Buckingham Palace Road
London
SW1W 0SR
United Kingdom
44-20-7333-0800
stadler@uk.adventinternational.com

Director Ron Sheldon
Advent International plc
111 Buckingham Palace Road
London
SW1W 0SR
United Kingdom
44-20-7333-0800
rsheldon@uk.adventinternational.com

Director Bruce Barclay
Advent International plc
111 Buckingham Palace Road
London
SW1W 0SR
United Kingdom
44-20-7333-0800
bbarclay@uk.adventinternational.com

VENTURE CAPITAL DIRECTORY

Managing Director Humphrey Battcock
Advent International plc
111 Buckingham Palace Road
London
SW1W 0SR
United Kingdom
44-20-7333-0800
hbattcock@uk.adventinternational.com

Director John Bernstein
Advent International plc
111 Buckingham Palace Road
London
SW1W 0SR
United Kingdom
44-20-7333-0800
jbernstein@uk.adventinternational.com

Director Fred Wakeman
Advent International plc
111 Buckingham Palace Road
London
SW1W 0SR
United Kingdom
44-20-7333-0800
fwakeman@uk.adventinternational.com

Director James Brocklebank
Advent International plc
111 Buckingham Palace Road
London
SW1W 0SR
United Kingdom
44-20-7333-0800
jbrocklebank@uk.adventinternational.com

Director Tim Franks
Advent International plc
111 Buckingham Palace Road
London
SW1W 0SR
United Kingdom
44-20-7333-0800
tfranks@uk.adventinternational.com

Principal Joanna Kirby

VENTURE CAPITAL DIRECTORY

Advent International plc
111 Buckingham Palace Road
London
SW1W 0SR
United Kingdom
44-20-7333-0800
jkirby@uk.adventinternational.com

Managing Director Eric Adjoubel
Advent International S.A.R.L.
8-10 rue Lamennais
FR-75008 Paris
France
33-1-5537-2900
eadjoubel@adventinternational.fr

Principal Guillaume Darbon
Advent International S.A.R.L.
8-10 rue Lamennais
FR-75008 Paris
France
33-1-5537-2900
gdarbon@adventinternational.fr

Principal Cédric Chateau
Advent International S.A.R.L.
8-10 rue Lamennais
FR-75008 Paris
France
33-1-5537-2900
cchateau@adventinternational.fr

Director Pascal Stefani
Advent International S.A.R.L.
8-10 rue Lamennais
FR-75008 Paris
France
33-1-5537-2900
pstefani@adventinternational.fr

Senior Associate Damien Lestang-Hourcastagné
Advent International S.A.R.L.
8-10 rue Lamennais
FR-75008 Paris
France
33-1-5537-2900

VENTURE CAPITAL DIRECTORY

dlestang@adventinternational.fr

Associate Héloïse Temple-Boyer
Advent International S.A.R.L.
8-10 rue Lamennais
FR-75008 Paris
France
33-1-5537-2900
htemple@adventinternational.fr

President Francis L'Esperance III
Agawam Partners LLC
300 Park Avenue
17th Floor
New York, New York 10022
212-717-2541
FAL@agawampartners.com

Mark Long
Aidant Capital
2110 Main Street
Suite 200
Santa Monica, California 90405
310-399-5800
mlong@aidant.com

Managing Director Adam Dolinko
Aidant Capital
2110 Main Street
Suite 200
Santa Monica, California 90405
310-399-5800
adolinko@aidant.com

Ivan Ivankovich
Aidant Capital
2110 Main Street
Suite 200
Santa Monica, California 90405
310-399-5800
iivankovich@aidant.com

Bill Nash
Aidant Capital
2110 Main Street
Suite 200

VENTURE CAPITAL DIRECTORY

Santa Monica, California 90405
310-399-5800
bnash@aidant.com

Principal Christopher Allen
Alacrity Ventures
1563 Solano Avenue, #353
Berkeley, California 94707-2116
510-649-4030
christophera@alacrityventures.com

Principal Gifford Pinchot
Alacrity Ventures
1563 Solano Avenue, #353
Berkeley, California 94707-2116
510-649-4030
giffordp@alacrityventures.com

Principal Harold Shattuck
Alacrity Ventures
1563 Solano Avenue, #353
Berkeley, California 94707-2116
510-649-4030
harolds@alacrityventures.com

Managing Partner Mark Arnold
Albion Investors LLC
75 Rockefeller Plaza
15th Floor
New York, New York 10019-6901
212-277-7520

Managing Partner Alastair Tedford
Albion Investors LLC
75 Rockefeller Plaza
15th Floor
New York, New York 10019-6901
212-277-7520

Managing Director Charles Gonzalez
Albion Investors LLC
75 Rockefeller Plaza
15th Floor
New York, New York 10019-6901
212-277-7520

VENTURE CAPITAL DIRECTORY

Managing Director Basil Livanos
Albion Investors LLC
75 Rockefeller Plaza
15th Floor
New York, New York 10019-6901
212-277-7520
blivanos@albioninvestors.com

Senior Vice President Arthur Meehan
Albion Investors LLC
75 Rockefeller Plaza
15th Floor
New York, New York 10019-6901
212-277-7520

Managing Director James Pendergast
Albion Investors LLC
75 Rockefeller Plaza
15th Floor
New York, New York 10019-6901
212-277-7520

Assistant Vice President Christine Gilhooley
Albion Investors LLC
75 Rockefeller Plaza
15th Floor
New York, New York 10019-6901
212-277-7520
cgilhooley@albioninvestors.com

Vice President Michael Spivak
Albion Investors LLC
75 Rockefeller Plaza
15th Floor
New York, New York 10019-6901
212-277-7520

Assistant Vice President, Accounting Eugene Fouksman
Albion Investors LLC
75 Rockefeller Plaza
15th Floor
New York, New York 10019-6901
212-277-7520
efouksman@albioninvestors.com

Partner Bruce Failing

VENTURE CAPITAL DIRECTORY

Alerion Partners
105 Rowayton Avenue
Rowayton, Connecticut 6853
203-838-6700
failing@alerionpartners.com

Partner Michael Persky
Alerion Partners
105 Rowayton Avenue
Rowayton, Connecticut 6853
203-838-6700
persky@alerionpartners.com

Partner Harry Rein
Alerion Partners
105 Rowayton Avenue
Rowayton, Connecticut 6853
203-838-6700
rein@alerionpartners.com

Partner Norman Tsang
Alerion Partners
105 Rowayton Avenue
Rowayton, Connecticut 6853
203-838-6700
tsang@alerionpartners.com

Venture Partner Robert Cioffi
Alerion Partners
105 Rowayton Avenue
Rowayton, Connecticut 6853
203-838-6700
cioffi@alerionpartners.com

Managing Director Kent Johnson
Alexander Hutton Venture Partners, L.P.
1215 Fourth Avenue
Suite 900
Seattle, Washington 98161
206-341-9800
kjohnson@ahvp.com

Managing Director Jerry Keppler
Alexander Hutton Venture Partners, L.P.
1215 Fourth Avenue
Suite 900

VENTURE CAPITAL DIRECTORY

Seattle, Washington 98161
206-341-9800
jkeppler@ahvp.com

Managing Director Mark Klebanoff
Alexander Hutton Venture Partners, L.P.
1215 Fourth Avenue
Suite 900
Seattle, Washington 98161
206-341-9800
mklebanoff@ahvp.com

Managing Director Tom Johnston
Alexander Hutton Venture Partners, L.P.
1215 Fourth Avenue
Suite 900
Seattle, Washington 98161
206-341-9800
tomj@ahvp.com

Principal James Thompson
Alexander Hutton Venture Partners, L.P.
1215 Fourth Avenue
Suite 900
Seattle, Washington 98161
206-341-9800
jthompson@ahvp.com

Organizational Psychologist Paul Tomlinson
Alexander Hutton Venture Partners, L.P.
1215 Fourth Avenue
Suite 900
Seattle, Washington 98161
206-341-9800
pault@ahvp.com

Managing Partner Jan-Erik Hareid
Alliance Venture
Stranden 57, Aker Brygge
NO-0250 Oslo
Norway
47-22-94-4020
hareid@allianceventure.com

Partner Erling Maartmann-Moe
Alliance Venture

VENTURE CAPITAL DIRECTORY

Stranden 57, Aker Brygge
NO-0250 Oslo
Norway
47-22-94-4020
erling@allianceventure.com

Partner Bjørn Christensen
Alliance Venture
Stranden 57, Aker Brygge
NO-0250 Oslo
Norway
47-22-94-4020
bjorn@allianceventure.com

Chairman and CEO William Walton
Allied Capital Corporation
401 North Michigan Avenue
Suite 2050
Chicago, Illinois 60611
312-846-5100

COO Joan Sweeney
Allied Capital Corporation
401 North Michigan Avenue
Suite 2050
Chicago, Illinois 60611
312-846-5100

Chief Valuation Officer Scott Binder
Allied Capital Corporation
1919 Pennsylvania Avenue, NW
Washington, District of Columbia 20006
202-721-6100
sbinder@alliedcapital.com

Managing Director Robert Long
Allied Capital Corporation
520 Madison Avenue
27th Floor
New York, New York 10022
212-822-7800
rlong@alliedcapital.com

VENTURE CAPITAL DIRECTORY

Managing Director Christina DelDonna
Allied Capital Corporation
1919 Pennsylvania Avenue, NW
Washington, District of Columbia 20006
202-721-6100

Managing Director John Shulman
Allied Capital Corporation
1919 Pennsylvania Avenue, NW
Washington, District of Columbia 20006
202-721-6100
jshulman@alliedcapital.com

Managing Director Michael Grisius
Allied Capital Corporation
1919 Pennsylvania Avenue, NW
Washington, District of Columbia 20006
202-721-6100
mgrisius@alliedcapital.com

Managing Director Jeri Harman
Allied Capital Corporation
11111 Santa Monica Boulevard
Los Angeles, California 90025
310-689-2800
jharman@alliedcapital.com

CFO Penni Roll
Allied Capital Corporation
1919 Pennsylvania Avenue, NW
Washington, District of Columbia 20006
202-721-6100

Managing Director George Ferris
Allied Capital Corporation
1919 Pennsylvania Avenue, NW
Washington, District of Columbia 20006
202-721-6100
gferris@alliedcapital.com

Managing Director Benton Cummings
Allied Capital Corporation
520 Madison Avenue
27th Floor
New York, New York 10022
212-822-7800

VENTURE CAPITAL DIRECTORY

bcummings@alliedcapital.com

President Andrew Kalnow
Alpha Capital Partners Ltd.
122 South Michigan Avenue
Suite 1700
Chicago, Illinois 60603
312-322-9800
ahkalnow@alphacapital.com

Managing Director Richard Goff
Alpha Capital Partners Ltd.
2593 Walnut Road
Ann Arbor, Michigan 48103
734-994-1003
rgoff@alphacapital.com

Managing Director Gary Stark
Alpha Capital Partners Ltd.
122 South Michigan Avenue
Suite 1700
Chicago, Illinois 60603
312-322-9800
garystark@alphacapital.com

Chairman J. Dirk Vos
Alpha Capital Partners Ltd.
122 South Michigan Avenue
Suite 1700
Chicago, Illinois 60603
312-322-9800
dvos@alphacapital.com

Senior Advisor Orval Cook
Alpha Capital Partners Ltd.
3155 Research Blvd.
Dayton, Ohio 45420
937-294-6938
ocook@alphcap.com

Managing General Partner Timothy Dibble
Alta Communications, Inc.
200 Clarendon Street
51st Floor
Boston, Massachusetts 2116
617-262-7770

VENTURE CAPITAL DIRECTORY

tdibble@altacomm.com

Managing General Partner Brian McNeill
Alta Communications, Inc.
200 Clarendon Street
51st Floor
Boston, Massachusetts 2116
617-262-7770
bmcneill@altacomm.com

General Partner William Egan
Alta Communications, Inc.
200 Clarendon Street
51st Floor
Boston, Massachusetts 2116
617-262-7770
began@altacomm.com

General Partner B. Lane MacDonald
Alta Communications, Inc.
200 Clarendon Street
51st Floor
Boston, Massachusetts 2116
617-262-7770
lmacdonald@altacomm.com

General Partner Robert Emmert
Alta Communications, Inc.
200 Clarendon Street
51st Floor
Boston, Massachusetts 2116
617-262-7770
bemmert@altacomm.com

General Partner Philip Thompson
Alta Communications, Inc.
200 Clarendon Street
51st Floor
Boston, Massachusetts 2116
617-262-7770
pthompson@altacomm.com

General Partner Patrick Brubaker
Alta Communications, Inc.
200 Clarendon Street
51st Floor
Boston, Massachusetts 2116

VENTURE CAPITAL DIRECTORY

617-262-7770
pbrubaker@altacomm.com

General Partner Andrew Mulderry
Alta Communications, Inc.
200 Clarendon Street
51st Floor
Boston, Massachusetts 2116
617-262-7770
amulderry@altacomm.com

General Partner Eileen McCarthy
Alta Communications, Inc.
200 Clarendon Street
51st Floor
Boston, Massachusetts 2116
617-262-7770
emccarthy@altacomm.com

Vice President Wayne Mack
Alta Communications, Inc.
200 Clarendon Street
51st Floor
Boston, Massachusetts 2116
617-262-7770
wmack@altacomm.com

Vice President Matthew Blodgett
Alta Communications, Inc.
200 Clarendon Street
51st Floor
Boston, Massachusetts 2116
617-262-7770
mblodgett@altacomm.com

Associate Alex Rosenfeld
Alta Communications, Inc.
200 Clarendon Street
51st Floor
Boston, Massachusetts 2116
617-262-7770
arosenfeld@altacomm.com

Associate Imran Ali
Alta Communications, Inc.
200 Clarendon Street

VENTURE CAPITAL DIRECTORY

51st Floor
Boston, Massachusetts 2116
617-262-7770
iali@altacomm.com

Associate Phillip Dudley
Alta Communications, Inc.
200 Clarendon Street
51st Floor
Boston, Massachusetts 2116
617-262-7770
pdudley@altacomm.com

Associate Todd Ruggini
Alta Communications, Inc.
200 Clarendon Street
51st Floor
Boston, Massachusetts 2116
617-262-7770
truggini@altacomm.com

Associate Jessica Barry
Alta Communications, Inc.
200 Clarendon Street
51st Floor
Boston, Massachusetts 2116
617-262-7770
jbarry@altacomm.com

Founding Partner Guillaume Aubin
Alven Capital
97, rue Réaumur
FR-75002 Paris
France
33-1-5534-3838
aubin@alvencapital.com

Founding Partner Charles Letourneur
Alven Capital
97, rue Réaumur
FR-75002 Paris
France
33-1-5534-3838

Partner Nicolas Celier
Alven Capital

VENTURE CAPITAL DIRECTORY

97, rue Réaumur
FR-75002 Paris
France
33-1-5534-3838

CFO Julie Barchilon
Alven Capital
97, rue Réaumur
FR-75002 Paris
France
33-1-5534-3838

Chief Executive Anne Glover
Amadeus Capital Partners Ltd.
Mount Pleasant House
2 Mount Pleasant
Cambridge
CB3 0RN
United Kingdom
44-1223-707-000
aglover@amadeuscapital.com

Director Hermann Hauser
Amadeus Capital Partners Ltd.
Mount Pleasant House
2 Mount Pleasant
Cambridge
CB3 0RN
United Kingdom
44-1223-707-000
hhauser@amadeuscapital.com

Partner Roy Merritt
Amadeus Capital Partners Ltd.
Mount Pleasant House
2 Mount Pleasant
Cambridge
CB3 0RN
United Kingdom
44-1223-707-000

CEO Amadeus Mobile Seed Fund Laurence John
Amadeus Capital Partners Ltd.
Mount Pleasant House
2 Mount Pleasant
Cambridge

VENTURE CAPITAL DIRECTORY

CB3 0RN
United Kingdom
44-1223-707-000

Director Richard Anton
Amadeus Capital Partners Ltd.
Mount Pleasant House
2 Mount Pleasant
Cambridge
CB3 0RN
United Kingdom
44-1223-707-000

Partner Simon Cornwell
Amadeus Capital Partners Ltd.
Mount Pleasant House
2 Mount Pleasant
Cambridge
CB3 0RN
United Kingdom
44-1223-707-000

Partner Andrea Traversone
Amadeus Capital Partners Ltd.
Mount Pleasant House
2 Mount Pleasant
Cambridge
CB3 0RN
United Kingdom
44-1223-707-000
andrea.traversone@amadeuscapital.com

Partner Barak Maoz
Amadeus Capital Partners Ltd.
Mount Pleasant House
2 Mount Pleasant
Cambridge
CB3 0RN
United Kingdom
44-1223-707-000

CEO Kenneth Anderson
Anderson Pacific Corporation
31st Floor, John Hancock Center
875 North Michigan Avenue
Chicago, Illinois 60611

VENTURE CAPITAL DIRECTORY

312-951-8500
kda@andersonpacific.com

Partner Adrian Beecroft
Apax Partners
15 Portland Place
London
W1B 1PT
United Kingdom
44-20-7872-6300
adrian.beecroft@apax.com

Partner Peter Englander
Apax Partners
15 Portland Place
London
W1B 1PT
United Kingdom
44-20-7872-6300
peter.englander@apax.com

Partner Paul Fitzsimons
Apax Partners
15 Portland Place
London
W1B 1PT
United Kingdom
44-20-7872-6300

Partner Michael Grabiner
Apax Partners
15 Portland Place
London
W1B 1PT
United Kingdom
44-20-7872-6300

Partner Stephen Grabiner
Apax Partners
15 Portland Place
London
W1B 1PT
United Kingdom
44-20-7872-6300
stephen.grabiner@apax.com

VENTURE CAPITAL DIRECTORY

Partner Stephen Green
Apax Partners
15 Portland Place
London
W1B 1PT
United Kingdom
44-20-7872-6300

Partner John McMonigall
Apax Partners
15 Portland Place
London
W1B 1PT
United Kingdom
44-20-7872-6300

Partner Ian Jones
Apax Partners
15 Portland Place
London
W1B 1PT
United Kingdom
44-20-7872-6300

Partner Emilio Voli
Apax Partners
15 Portland Place
London
W1B 1PT
United Kingdom
44-20-7872-6300
emilio.voli@apax.com

Partner Lars Johansson
Apax Partners AB
Birger Jarlsgatan 5
SE-11145 Stockholm
Sweden
46-8-545-074-00
lars.johansson@apax.com

Apax Partners Beteiligungsberatung GmbH
Partner Michael Phillips
Possartstrasse 11
Kopernikusstrasse
DE-81679 Munich

VENTURE CAPITAL DIRECTORY

Germany
49-89-998-9090
michael.phillips@apax.de

Apax Partners Beteiligungsberatung GmbH
Partner Christian Näther
Possartstrasse 11
Kopernikusstrasse
DE-81679 Munich
Germany
49-89-998-9090

Apax Partners Beteiligungsberatung GmbH
Partner Torsten Krumm
Possartstrasse 11
Kopernikusstrasse
DE-81679 Munich
Germany
49-89-998-9090
torsten.krumm@apax.de

Partner Nicolás Bonilla
Apax Partners España S.A.
Velázquez, 10-5°
ES-28001 Madrid
Spain
34-91-423-1000
nicolas.bonilla@apax.com

Principal Borja Martínez
Apax Partners España S.A.
Velázquez, 10-5°
ES-28001 Madrid
Spain
34-91-423-1000
borja.martinez@apax.com

Hong Kong

19th Floor, One International Finance CentreNo.1 Harbour View Street, Central
Apax Partners Hong Kong Ltd.
 Burger-CalderonMax
852-2166-8230

Hong Kong

VENTURE CAPITAL DIRECTORY

19th Floor, One International Finance CentreNo.1 Harbour View Street, Central
Apax Partners Hong Kong Ltd.
 PrahlMichael
852-2166-8230

Zehavit Cohen
Apax Partners (Israel) Ltd.
Museum Tower
4 Berkowitz Street
Tel Aviv 64238
Israel
972-3-777-4410
zehavit.cohen@apax.com

Gal Hayut
Apax Partners (Israel) Ltd.
Museum Tower
4 Berkowitz Street
Tel Aviv 64238
Israel
972-3-777-4410

Pinchas Barel Buchris
Apax Partners (Israel) Ltd.
Museum Tower
4 Berkowitz Street
Tel Aviv 64238
Israel
972-3-777-4410

CEO John Megrue Jr.
Apax Partners, L.P.
153 East 53rd Street
53rd Floor
New York, New York 10022
212-753-6300
john.megrue@apax.com

Partner Oren Zeev
Apax Partners, L.P.
153 East 53rd Street
53rd Floor
New York, New York 10022
212-753-6300
oren.zeev@apax.com

VENTURE CAPITAL DIRECTORY

Partner Mitch Truwit
Apax Partners, L.P.
153 East 53rd Street
53rd Floor
New York, New York 10022
212-753-6300
mitch.truwit@apax.com

COO Peter Jeton
Apax Partners, L.P.
153 East 53rd Street
53rd Floor
New York, New York 10022
212-753-6300

Partner Jacqueline Reses
Apax Partners, L.P.
153 East 53rd Street
53rd Floor
New York, New York 10022
212-753-6300

Partner David Kim
Apax Partners, L.P.
153 East 53rd Street
53rd Floor
New York, New York 10022
212-753-6300
david.kim@apax.com

Partner Buddy Gumina
Apax Partners, L.P.
153 East 53rd Street
53rd Floor
New York, New York 10022
212-753-6300
buddy.gumina@apax.com

Managing Director Giancarlo Aliberti
Apax Partners S.r.l.
Palazzo Gallarati Scotti
IT-20121 Milan
Italy
39-2-762119-1
giancarlo.aliberti@apax.com

VENTURE CAPITAL DIRECTORY

Partner Amedeo Carassai
Apax Partners S.r.l.
Palazzo Gallarati Scotti
IT-20121 Milan
Italy
39-2-762119-1

David Schwartz
Apropos IT Ventures
Jerusalem Technology Park, Malcha
Building 1, Entrance B, 1st Floor, P.O. Box 48180
Jerusalem 91481
Israel
972-2-648-2350
dschwartz@aitventures.com

Jerry Zucker
Apropos IT Ventures
Jerusalem Technology Park, Malcha
Building 1, Entrance B, 1st Floor, P.O. Box 48180
Jerusalem 91481
Israel
972-2-648-2350
jzucker@aitventures.com

Joseph Gellman
Apropos IT Ventures
Jerusalem Technology Park, Malcha
Building 1, Entrance B, 1st Floor, P.O. Box 48180
Jerusalem 91481
Israel
972-2-648-2350
jbgellman@aitventures.com

Co-Founder and Managing Director Keith Crandell
ARCH Venture Partners
8725 West Higgins Road
Suite 290
Chicago, Illinois 60631
773-380-6600
klc@archventure.com

Co-Founder and Managing Director, Emeritus Steven Lazarus
ARCH Venture Partners
8725 West Higgins Road
Suite 290

VENTURE CAPITAL DIRECTORY

Chicago, Illinois 60631
773-380-6600
sl@archventure.com

Co-Founder and Managing Director Robert Nelsen
ARCH Venture Partners
1000 Second Avenue
Suite 3700
Seattle, Washington 98104
206-674-3028
rtn@archventure.com

Co-Founder and Managing Director Clinton Bybee
ARCH Venture Partners
6300 Bridgepoint Parkway
Building One, Suite 500
Austin, Texas 78730
512-795-5830
cwb@archventure.com

Managing Director Patrick Ennis
ARCH Venture Partners
1000 Second Avenue
Suite 3700
Seattle, Washington 98104
206-674-3028
pjennis@archventure.com

Managing Director Scott Minick
ARCH Venture Partners
1000 Second Avenue
Suite 3700
Seattle, Washington 98104
206-674-3028
sminick@archventure.com

Principal Paul Thurk
ARCH Venture Partners
6300 Bridgepoint Parkway
Building One, Suite 500
Austin, Texas 78730
512-795-5830
pthurk@archventure.com

Principal Michael Janse
ARCH Venture Partners

VENTURE CAPITAL DIRECTORY

8725 West Higgins Road
Suite 290
Chicago, Illinois 60631
773-380-6600
mjanse@archventure.com

Principal Kristina Burow
ARCH Venture Partners
8725 West Higgins Road
Suite 290
Chicago, Illinois 60631
773-380-6600
kburow@archventure.com

Venture Partner Edgar Hotard
ARCH Venture Partners
8725 West Higgins Road
Suite 290
Chicago, Illinois 60631
773-380-6600
ehotard@archventure.com

Managing Director Steven Gillis
ARCH Venture Partners
1000 Second Avenue
Suite 3700
Seattle, Washington 98104
206-674-3028
sgillis@archventure.com

Venture Partner Hong Hou
ARCH Venture Partners
2325 Third Street
Suite 407
San Francisco, California 94107
415-565-7103
hhou@archventure.com

Venture Partner Don Oliverio
ARCH Venture Partners
6300 Bridgepoint Parkway
Building One, Suite 500
Austin, Texas 78730
512-795-5830
doliverio@archventure.com

VENTURE CAPITAL DIRECTORY

Managing Director Stevan Birnbaum
Arcturus Capital
350 West Colorado Blvd.
Suite 215
Pasadena, California 91105
626-578-5700
sbirnbaum@arcturusvc.com

Managing Director Donald Hall
Arcturus Capital
350 West Colorado Blvd.
Suite 215
Pasadena, California 91105
626-578-5700
dhall@arcturusvc.com

Managing Director Stephen Watkins
Arcturus Capital
350 West Colorado Blvd.
Suite 215
Pasadena, California 91105
626-578-5700
stephen@arcturusvc.com

Venture Partner Edwin Moss
Arcturus Capital
350 West Colorado Blvd.
Suite 215
Pasadena, California 91105
626-578-5700
emoss@arcturusvc.com

Venture Partner John Baldeschwieler
Arcturus Capital
350 West Colorado Blvd.
Suite 215
Pasadena, California 91105
626-578-5700
john@arcturusvc.com

Associate Darin Chen
Arcturus Capital
350 West Colorado Blvd.
Suite 215
Pasadena, California 91105
626-578-5700

VENTURE CAPITAL DIRECTORY

darin@arcturusvc.com

Executive in Residence Henry DeNero
Arcturus Capital
350 West Colorado Blvd.
Suite 215
Pasadena, California 91105
626-578-5700
henry@arcturusvc.com

Venture Partner Amnon Yariv
Arcturus Capital
350 West Colorado Blvd.
Suite 215
Pasadena, California 91105
626-578-5700
amnon@arcturusvc.com

CEO Julie Meyer
Ariadne Capital
28 Queen Street
London
EC4R 1BB
United Kingdom
44-20-7653-0204
julie@ariadnecapital.com

General Partner Michael Granger
Ark Capital Management
150 North Wacker Drive
Suite 2360
Chicago, Illinois 60606
312-541-0330
michael@arkvc.com

General Partner Xcylur Stoakley
Ark Capital Management
150 North Wacker Drive
Suite 2360
Chicago, Illinois 60606
312-541-0330
xcylur@arkvc.com

Partner Raymond Smith
Arlington Capital Partners
600 New Hampshire Ave., NW

VENTURE CAPITAL DIRECTORY

Suite 660
Washington, District of Columbia 20037
202-337-7500
reighsmith@aol.com

Founding Partner Robert Knibb
Arlington Capital Partners
600 New Hampshire Ave., NW
Suite 660
Washington, District of Columbia 20037
202-337-7500
rknibb@arlingtoncap.com

Founding Partner Jeffrey Freed
Arlington Capital Partners
600 New Hampshire Ave., NW
Suite 660
Washington, District of Columbia 20037
202-337-7500
jfreed@arlingtoncap.com

Managing Director Perry Steiner
Arlington Capital Partners
600 New Hampshire Ave., NW
Suite 660
Washington, District of Columbia 20037
202-337-7500
psteiner@arlingtoncap.com

Vice President John Bates
Arlington Capital Partners
600 New Hampshire Ave., NW
Suite 660
Washington, District of Columbia 20037
202-337-7500
jbates@arlingtoncap.com

Partner Peter Manos
Arlington Capital Partners
600 New Hampshire Ave., NW
Suite 660
Washington, District of Columbia 20037
202-337-7500
pmanos@arlingtoncap.com

Vice President Michael Lustbader

VENTURE CAPITAL DIRECTORY

Arlington Capital Partners
600 New Hampshire Ave., NW
Suite 660
Washington, District of Columbia 20037
202-337-7500
mlustbader@arlingtoncap.com

Vice President Matthew Altman
Arlington Capital Partners
600 New Hampshire Ave., NW
Suite 660
Washington, District of Columbia 20037
202-337-7500
maltman@arlingtoncap.com

Jesse Liu
Arlington Capital Partners
600 New Hampshire Ave., NW
Suite 660
Washington, District of Columbia 20037
202-337-7500
jliu@arlingtoncap.com

Associate Matthew Rich
Arlington Capital Partners
600 New Hampshire Ave., NW
Suite 660
Washington, District of Columbia 20037
202-337-7500
mrich@arlingtoncap.com

CFO Matthew Buckley
Arlington Capital Partners
600 New Hampshire Ave., NW
Suite 660
Washington, District of Columbia 20037
202-337-7500
mbuckley@arlingtoncap.com

Edward Weklar
Arlington Capital Partners
600 New Hampshire Ave., NW
Suite 660
Washington, District of Columbia 20037
202-337-7500
eweklar@arlingtoncap.com

VENTURE CAPITAL DIRECTORY

Managing Partner Thomas Hoegh
Arts Alliance Ltd.
5 Young Street
London
W8 5EH
United Kingdom
44-20-7361-7720
thomas@artsalliance.co.uk

Managing Partner Laurent Laffy
Arts Alliance Ltd.
5 Young Street
London
W8 5EH
United Kingdom
44-20-7361-7720

Venture Partner Victoria Hackett
Arts Alliance Ltd.
5 Young Street
London
W8 5EH
United Kingdom
44-20-7361-7720

Partner Adam Valkin
Arts Alliance Ltd.
5 Young Street
London
W8 5EH
United Kingdom
44-20-7361-7720
adam@artsalliance.co.uk

Principal Joshua Green
Arts Alliance Ltd.
5 Young Street
London
W8 5EH
United Kingdom
44-20-7361-7720

Managing Director Christopher Dick
Ascent Venture Partners
255 State Street
5th Floor

VENTURE CAPITAL DIRECTORY

Boston, Massachusetts 2109
617-720-9400
cwdick@ascentvp.com

Managing Director Christopher Lynch
Ascent Venture Partners
255 State Street
5th Floor
Boston, Massachusetts 2109
617-720-9400
clynch@ascentvp.com

Special Limited Partner Frank Polestra
Ascent Venture Partners
255 State Street
5th Floor
Boston, Massachusetts 2109
617-720-9400

Partner and CFO Brian Girvan
Ascent Venture Partners
255 State Street
5th Floor
Boston, Massachusetts 2109
617-720-9400
bgirvan@ascentvp.com

Partner Geoffrey Oblak
Ascent Venture Partners
255 State Street
5th Floor
Boston, Massachusetts 2109
617-720-9400
goblak@ascentvp.com

Principal Matt Fates
Ascent Venture Partners
255 State Street
5th Floor
Boston, Massachusetts 2109
617-720-9400
mfates@ascentvp.com

Senior Associate Luke Burns
Ascent Venture Partners
255 State Street

VENTURE CAPITAL DIRECTORY

5th Floor
Boston, Massachusetts 2109
617-720-9400
lburns@ascentvp.com

Hong Kong

17th Floor, China Hong Kong Tower 8-12 Hennessy Road
Asia Capital Management Ltd.
 BowenLouis
852-2525-8151
louis@acmhk.com

Hong Kong

17th Floor, China Hong Kong Tower 8-12 Hennessy Road
Asia Capital Management Ltd.
 Collins-TaylorJames
852-2525-8151
james@acmhk.com

Hong Kong

17th Floor, China Hong Kong Tower 8-12 Hennessy Road
Asia Capital Management Ltd.
 ChengRonie
852-2525-8151
ronie@acmhk.com

Hong Kong

26/F, Nine Queen's Road Central
Asia Pacific Capital (HK) Ltd.
McAfeeGage
852-2801-5993
gage@geapctechfund.com

Hong Kong

26/F, Nine Queen's Road Central
Asia Pacific Capital (HK) Ltd.
 KothariAshok
852-2801-5993
ashok@geapctechfund.com

Hong Kong

VENTURE CAPITAL DIRECTORY

26/F, Nine Queen's Road Central
Asia Pacific Capital (HK) Ltd.
 LienSean
852-2801-5993

Hong Kong

26/F, Nine Queen's Road Central
Asia Pacific Capital (HK) Ltd.
 EastmanAlicia
852-2801-5993

Hong Kong

26/F, Nine Queen's Road Central
Asia Pacific Capital (HK) Ltd.
 HongWong
852-2801-5993

Hong Kong

26/F, Nine Queen's Road Central
Asia Pacific Capital (HK) Ltd.
 LiuMichael
852-2801-5993

Founding Partner Dominique Oger
AtriA Capital Partenaires
40, rue de Chateaudun
FR-75009 Paris
France
33-1-4526-6016
d.oger@atria-partenaires.com

Founding Partner Patrick Lente
AtriA Capital Partenaires
40, rue de Chateaudun
FR-75009 Paris
France
33-1-4526-6016
p.lente@atria-partenaires.com

Founding Partner Patrick Bertiaux
AtriA Capital Partenaires
40, rue de Chateaudun

VENTURE CAPITAL DIRECTORY

FR-75009 Paris
France
33-1-4526-6016
p.bertiaux@atria-partenaires.com

Co-CEO Geoffrey Rehnert
Audax Private Equity
101 Huntington Avenue
Boston, Massachusetts 2199
617-859-1500
grehnert@audaxgroup.com

Managing Partner Richard Green
August Equity LLP
10 Bedford Street
London
WC2E 9HE
United Kingdom
44-20-7632-8200
richard.green@augustequity.com

Aura Capital Oy
Managing Partner Ari Siponmaa
Kluuvikatu 5
FI-00100 Helsinki
Finland
358-10-8300-600
ari.siponmaa@auratum.com

Australasian Media & Communications Fund
Tim Downing
Level 6
175 Macquarie Street
Sydney New South Wales 2000
Australia
61-2-9235-1100
tdowning@amcf.com.au

Managing Partner David Unger
Avalon Equity Partners
800 Third Avenue
27th Floor
New York, New York 10022
212-421-0600
dunger@avalonequity.com

VENTURE CAPITAL DIRECTORY

Managing Partner Benjamin Brandes
Avalon Equity Partners
800 Third Avenue
27th Floor
New York, New York 10022
212-421-0600
bbrandes@avalonequity.com

CFO Peter Polimino
Avalon Equity Partners
800 Third Avenue
27th Floor
New York, New York 10022
212-421-0600
ppolimino@avalonequity.com

Controller Alan Shum
Avalon Equity Partners
800 Third Avenue
27th Floor
New York, New York 10022
212-421-0600
ashum@avalonequity.com

Co-Managing Partner and CEO Thompson Dean
Avista Capital Partners
65 East 55th Street
18th Floor
New York, New York 10022
212-593-6900

Co-Managing Partner and President Steven Webster
Avista Capital Partners
65 East 55th Street
18th Floor
New York, New York 10022
212-593-6900

Partner David Burgstahler
Avista Capital Partners
65 East 55th Street
18th Floor
New York, New York 10022
212-593-6900

Partner David Durkin

VENTURE CAPITAL DIRECTORY

Avista Capital Partners
65 East 55th Street
18th Floor
New York, New York 10022
212-593-6900

Industry Partner James Finkelstein
Avista Capital Partners
65 East 55th Street
18th Floor
New York, New York 10022
212-593-6900

Partner OhSang Kwon
Avista Capital Partners
65 East 55th Street
18th Floor
New York, New York 10022
212-593-6900

Industry Partner Larry Pickering
Avista Capital Partners
65 East 55th Street
18th Floor
New York, New York 10022
212-593-6900

Partner Robert Cabes
Avista Capital Partners
65 East 55th Street
18th Floor
New York, New York 10022
212-593-6900

Managing Director Josh Bekenstein
Bain Capital, Inc.
111 Huntington Avenue
Boston, Massachusetts 2199
617-516-2000
jbekenstein@baincapital.com

Managing Director Ed Conard
Bain Capital, Inc.
111 Huntington Avenue
Boston, Massachusetts 2199
617-516-2000

VENTURE CAPITAL DIRECTORY

econard@baincapital.com

Managing Director John Connaughton
Bain Capital, Inc.
111 Huntington Avenue
Boston, Massachusetts 2199
617-516-2000
jconnaughton@baincapital.com

Managing Director Paul Edgerley
Bain Capital, Inc.
111 Huntington Avenue
Boston, Massachusetts 2199
617-516-2000
pedgerley@baincapital.com

Managing Director Mark Nunnelly
Bain Capital, Inc.
111 Huntington Avenue
Boston, Massachusetts 2199
617-516-2000
mnunnelly@baincapital.com

Partner Henry Baker
Baker Capital Corporation
540 Madison Avenue
29th Floor
New York, New York 10022
212-848-2000
hbaker@bakercapital.com

Partner John Baker
Baker Capital Corporation
540 Madison Avenue
29th Floor
New York, New York 10022
212-848-2000
jbaker@bakercapital.com

Partner Jonathan Grabel
Baker Capital Corporation
540 Madison Avenue
29th Floor
New York, New York 10022
212-848-2000

VENTURE CAPITAL DIRECTORY

Partner P. Kevin Kilroy
Baker Capital Corporation
540 Madison Avenue
29th Floor
New York, New York 10022
212-848-2000
kkilroy@bakercapital.com

Partner Faisal Nisar
Baker Capital Corporation
540 Madison Avenue
29th Floor
New York, New York 10022
212-848-2000

Partner Rob Manning
Baker Capital Corporation
540 Madison Avenue
29th Floor
New York, New York 10022
212-848-2000

Partner David Ruberg
Baker Capital Corporation
540 Madison Avenue
29th Floor
New York, New York 10022
212-848-2000

CFO Joseph Saviano
Baker Capital Corporation
540 Madison Avenue
29th Floor
New York, New York 10022
212-848-2000

Managing Partner Thomas M. Higgins
Balkan Accession Fund
3 Shipka Street
BU-1504 Sofia
Bulgaria
359-2-946-0119
tom.higgins@bafund.net

Partner Bistra D. Kirova
Balkan Accession Fund

VENTURE CAPITAL DIRECTORY

3 Shipka Street
BU-1504 Sofia
Bulgaria
359-2-946-0119
bistra.kirova@bafund.net

Managing Partner Horia Manda
Balkan Accession Fund
3 Aviatorilor Street
Sector 1
RO-011853 Bucharest
Romania
40-21-222-8501
horia.manda@bafund.net

Partner Roxana Vitan
Balkan Accession Fund
3 Aviatorilor Street
Sector 1
RO-011853 Bucharest
Romania
40-21-222-8501
roxana.vitan@bafund.net

Partner Neculai Sandu
Balkan Accession Fund
3 Aviatorilor Street
Sector 1
RO-011853 Bucharest
Romania
40-21-222-8501
neculai.sandu@bafund.net

Managing Partner Travis Hain
Banc of America Capital Investors
100 North Tryon Street
25th Floor
Charlotte, North Carolina 28255
704-386-4710
travis.hain@bankofamerica.com

Partner Rob Edwards
Banc of America Capital Investors
100 North Tryon Street
25th Floor
Charlotte, North Carolina 28255

VENTURE CAPITAL DIRECTORY

704-386-4710
robert.l.edwards@bankofamerica.com

Partner Craig Elson
Banc of America Capital Investors
100 North Tryon Street
25th Floor
Charlotte, North Carolina 28255
704-386-4710
craig.a.elson@bankofamerica.com

Partner Donny Harrison
Banc of America Capital Investors
100 North Tryon Street
25th Floor
Charlotte, North Carolina 28255
704-386-4710
donny.harrison@bankofamerica.com

Partner George Morgan
Banc of America Capital Investors
100 North Tryon Street
25th Floor
Charlotte, North Carolina 28255
704-386-4710
george.morgan@bankofamerica.com

Partner Scott Poole
Banc of America Capital Investors
100 North Tryon Street
25th Floor
Charlotte, North Carolina 28255
704-386-4710
scott.r.poole@bankofamerica.com

Partner Walker Poole
Banc of America Capital Investors
100 North Tryon Street
25th Floor
Charlotte, North Carolina 28255
704-386-4710
walker.l.poole@bankofamerica.com

Partner Trey Sheridan
Banc of America Capital Investors
100 North Tryon Street

VENTURE CAPITAL DIRECTORY

25th Floor
Charlotte, North Carolina 28255
704-386-4710
robert.sheridan@bankofamerica.com

Partner John Shimp
Banc of America Capital Investors
100 North Tryon Street
25th Floor
Charlotte, North Carolina 28255
704-386-4710
john.a.shimp@bankofamerica.com

Vice President Ryan Gable
Banc of America Capital Investors
100 North Tryon Street
25th Floor
Charlotte, North Carolina 28255
704-386-4710
ryan.l.gable@bankofamerica.com

Senior Associate Jack Purcell
Banc of America Capital Investors
100 North Tryon Street
25th Floor
Charlotte, North Carolina 28255
704-386-4710
jack.purcell@bankofamerica.com

Managing Director Kip Kapur
Barclays Ventures
1st Floor
15 Jermyn Street
London
SW1Y 6LT
United Kingdom
44-20-7445-3222
kip.kapur@barclays.com

Director Jeremy Morgan
Barclays Ventures
1st Floor
15 Jermyn Street
London
SW1Y 6LT
United Kingdom

VENTURE CAPITAL DIRECTORY

44-20-7445-3222
jeremy.morgan@barclays.com

Investment Director Andy Bate
Barclays Ventures
6th Floor
55 King Street
Manchester
M2 4LQ
United Kingdom
44-161-214-0818
andy.bate@barclays.com

Director Khilan Dodhia
Barclays Ventures
1st Floor
15 Jermyn Street
London
SW1Y 6LT
United Kingdom
44-20-7445-3222
khilan.dodhia@barclays.com

Partner Heather Potters
Baring Communications Equity (Emerging Europe) Capital Sp. z o.o.
Pulawska 17
Poludniowa Oficyna, III Floor
PL-02515 Warsaw
Poland
48-22-8811-640
potters@bce.pl

Partner Markus Pedriks
Baring Communications Equity (Emerging Europe) Capital Sp. z o.o.
Pulawska 17
Poludniowa Oficyna, III Floor
PL-02515 Warsaw
Poland
48-22-8811-640

Partner David French
Baring Communications Equity (Emerging Europe) Capital Sp. z o.o.
Pulawska 17
Poludniowa Oficyna, III Floor
PL-02515 Warsaw
Poland

VENTURE CAPITAL DIRECTORY

48-22-8811-640

Baring Vostok Capital Partners Ltd.
Calvey Michael
Ducat Place II, Suite 750
Moscow
Russia
RU-123056
7-495-967-1307
calvey@bvcp.ru

Baring Vostok Capital Partners Ltd.
Kalinin Alexei
Ducat Place II, Suite 750
Moscow
Russia
RU-123056
7-495-967-1307

Baring Vostok Capital Partners Ltd.
Broun Jean Michel
Ducat Place II, Suite 750
Moscow
Russia
RU-123056
7-495-967-1307
jmb@bvcp.ru

Baring Vostok Capital Partners Ltd.
Ivashentseva Elena
Ducat Place II, Suite 750
Moscow
Russia
RU-123056
7-495-967-1307

Baring Vostok Capital Partners Ltd.
Costyashkin Andrey
Ducat Place II, Suite 750
Moscow
Russia
RU-123056
7-495-967-1307

Baring Vostok Capital Partners Ltd.
Lomtadze Michael

VENTURE CAPITAL DIRECTORY

Ducat Place II, Suite 750
Moscow
Russia
RU-123056
7-495-967-1307
mlomtadze@bvcp.ru

Baring Vostok Capital Partners Ltd.
Der Megreditchian Philippe
Ducat Place II, Suite 750
Moscow
Russia
RU-123056
7-495-967-1307

President David Barry
Bariston Partners, LLC
225 Franklin Street
26th Floor
Boston, Massachusetts 2110
617-330-8950
dbarry@bariston.com

Managing Director Martin Madden
Bariston Partners, LLC
225 Franklin Street
26th Floor
Boston, Massachusetts 2110
617-330-8950

Managing Director Christopher Needham
Bariston Partners, LLC
225 Franklin Street
26th Floor
Boston, Massachusetts 2110
617-330-8950

Managing Director Patrick Alexander
Batavia Investment Management Ltd.
Plaza Bapindo, Tower II, Floor 12
Jl. Jenderal Sudirman, Kav 54-55
Jakarta 12190
Indonesia
62-21-524-6006

General Partner Tom Crotty

VENTURE CAPITAL DIRECTORY

Battery Ventures, L.P.
Reservoir Woods
930 Winter Street, Suite 2500
Waltham, Massachusetts 2451
781-478-6600
tom@battery.com

General Partner Ollie Curme
Battery Ventures, L.P.
Reservoir Woods
930 Winter Street, Suite 2500
Waltham, Massachusetts 2451
781-478-6600
ollie@battery.com

General Partner Richard Frisbie
Battery Ventures, L.P.
Reservoir Woods
930 Winter Street, Suite 2500
Waltham, Massachusetts 2451
781-478-6600
rick@battery.com

General Partner Scott Tobin
Battery Ventures, L.P.
Reservoir Woods
930 Winter Street, Suite 2500
Waltham, Massachusetts 2451
781-478-6600
scott@battery.com

General Partner Ken Lawler
Battery Ventures, L.P.
2884 Sand Hill Rd.
Suite 101
Menlo Park, California 94025
650-372-3939
ken@battery.com

General Partner Morgan Jones
Battery Ventures, L.P.
Reservoir Woods
930 Winter Street, Suite 2500
Waltham, Massachusetts 2451
781-478-6600
morgan@battery.com

VENTURE CAPITAL DIRECTORY

General Partner Mark Sherman
Battery Ventures, L.P.
2884 Sand Hill Rd.
Suite 101
Menlo Park, California 94025
650-372-3939
sherman@battery.com

General Partner David Tabors
Battery Ventures, L.P.
Reservoir Woods
930 Winter Street, Suite 2500
Waltham, Massachusetts 2451
781-478-6600
dave@battery.com

General Partner Roger Lee
Battery Ventures, L.P.
2884 Sand Hill Rd.
Suite 101
Menlo Park, California 94025
650-372-3939
roger@battery.com

Partner Neeraj Agrawal
Battery Ventures, L.P.
Reservoir Woods
930 Winter Street, Suite 2500
Waltham, Massachusetts 2451
781-478-6600
neeraj@battery.com

Partner Michael Brown
Battery Ventures, L.P.
Reservoir Woods
930 Winter Street, Suite 2500
Waltham, Massachusetts 2451
781-478-6600
michael@battery.com

Partner Cornel Faucher
Battery Ventures, L.P.
Reservoir Woods
930 Winter Street, Suite 2500
Waltham, Massachusetts 2451

VENTURE CAPITAL DIRECTORY

781-478-6600
cornel@battery.com

Partner Sunil Dhaliwal
Battery Ventures, L.P.
Reservoir Woods
930 Winter Street, Suite 2500
Waltham, Massachusetts 2451
781-478-6600
sunil@battery.com

Partner David Dreessen
Battery Ventures, L.P.
Reservoir Woods
930 Winter Street, Suite 2500
Waltham, Massachusetts 2451
781-478-6600
ddreessen@battery.com

Partner Jason Matlof
Battery Ventures, L.P.
Reservoir Woods
930 Winter Street, Suite 2500
Waltham, Massachusetts 2451
781-478-6600
jmatlof@battery.com

Partner Matt Niehaus
Battery Ventures, L.P.
2884 Sand Hill Rd.
Suite 101
Menlo Park, California 94025
650-372-3939
mniehaus@battery.com

Partner Mike Scanlin
Battery Ventures, L.P.
2884 Sand Hill Rd.
Suite 101
Menlo Park, California 94025
650-372-3939
mscanlin@battery.com

Executive Director Andra Sheffer
Bell Fund
2 Carlton St., Suite 1709

VENTURE CAPITAL DIRECTORY

Toronto Ontario M5B 1J3
Canada
416-977-8154

Associate Director Claire Dion
Bell Fund
4200, boul. Saint-Laurent, bureau 503
Montreal Quebec H2W 2R2
Canada
514-845-4418

CEO R. Chadwick Paul Jr.
Ben Franklin Technology Partners of Northeastern Pennsylvania
125 Goodman Drive
Bethlehem, Pennsylvania 18015-3715
610-758-5200
cpaul@nep.benfranklin.org

General Partner Alex Balkanski
Benchmark Capital
2480 Sand Hill Road
Suite 200
Menlo Park, California 94025
650-854-8180
abalkanski@benchmark.com

General Partner Bruce Dunlevie
Benchmark Capital
2480 Sand Hill Road
Suite 200
Menlo Park, California 94025
650-854-8180
bdunlevie@benchmark.com

General Partner Peter Fenton
Benchmark Capital
2480 Sand Hill Road
Suite 200
Menlo Park, California 94025
650-854-8180
pfenton@benchmark.com

General Partner Bill Gurley
Benchmark Capital
2480 Sand Hill Road
Suite 200

VENTURE CAPITAL DIRECTORY

Menlo Park, California 94025
650-854-8180
bgurley@benchmark.com

General Partner Kevin Harvey
Benchmark Capital
2480 Sand Hill Road
Suite 200
Menlo Park, California 94025
650-854-8180
kharvey@benchmark.com

General Partner Bob Kagle
Benchmark Capital
2480 Sand Hill Road
Suite 200
Menlo Park, California 94025
650-854-8180
rkagle@benchmark.com

General Partner Steve Spurlock
Benchmark Capital
2480 Sand Hill Road
Suite 200
Menlo Park, California 94025
650-854-8180
sspurlock@benchmark.com

Partner David Beirne
Benchmark Capital
2480 Sand Hill Road
Suite 200
Menlo Park, California 94025
650-854-8180
dbeirne@benchmark.com

Investment Director Jeff Bocan
Beringea LLC
39 Earlham Street
London
WC2H 9LT
United Kingdom
44-20-7845-7820
jbocan@beringea.co.uk

Senior Managing Director Charles Rothstein

VENTURE CAPITAL DIRECTORY

Beringea LLC
32330 W. 12 Mile Road
Farmington Hills, Michigan 48334
248-489-9000
crothstein@beringea.com

Senior Managing Director Malcolm Moss
Beringea LLC
32330 W. 12 Mile Road
Farmington Hills, Michigan 48334
248-489-9000
mmoss@beringea.com

Senior Managing Director Alexander Spiro Jr.
Beringea LLC
32330 W. 12 Mile Road
Farmington Hills, Michigan 48334
248-489-9000
aspiro@beringea.com

Berlin Capital Fund GmbH
Managing Director Clemens Kabel
Bundesallee 184/185
DE-10717 Berlin
Germany
49-30-8595-43-0
kabel@berlin-capitalfund.de

Berlin Capital Fund GmbH
Managing Director Stefan Beil
Bundesallee 184/185
DE-10717 Berlin
Germany
49-30-8595-43-0
beil@berlin-capitalfund.de

Berlin Capital Fund GmbH
Managing Director Peter Folle
Bundesallee 184/185
DE-10717 Berlin
Germany
49-30-8595-43-0

Berlin Capital Fund GmbH
Managing Director Johannes Rabini
Bundesallee 184/185

VENTURE CAPITAL DIRECTORY

DE-10717 Berlin
Germany
49-30-8595-43-0
rabini@berlin-capitalfund.de

Berlin Capital Fund GmbH
Senior Investment Manager Carsten Just
Bundesallee 184/185
DE-10717 Berlin
Germany
49-30-8595-43-0
just@berlin-capitalfund.de

Principal Llyod Sams
BIA Digital Partners, LP
15120 Enterprise Court
Suite 200
Chantilly, Virginia 20151
703-227-9600
lsams@bia.com

Principal Gregg Johnson
BIA Digital Partners, LP
15120 Enterprise Court
Suite 200
Chantilly, Virginia 20151
703-227-9600
gjohnson@bia.com

Principal Thomas Buono
BIA Digital Partners, LP
15120 Enterprise Court
Suite 200
Chantilly, Virginia 20151
703-227-9600
tbuono@bia.com

Principal Charles Wiebe
BIA Digital Partners, LP
15120 Enterprise Court
Suite 200
Chantilly, Virginia 20151
703-227-9600
cwiebe@bia.com

Director Scott Chappell

VENTURE CAPITAL DIRECTORY

BIA Digital Partners, LP
15120 Enterprise Court
Suite 200
Chantilly, Virginia 20151
703-227-9600
schappell@bia.com

Associate Damien Dovi
BIA Digital Partners, LP
15120 Enterprise Court
Suite 200
Chantilly, Virginia 20151
703-227-9600
ddovi@bia.com

CFO Clare Zecher
BIA Digital Partners, LP
15120 Enterprise Court
Suite 200
Chantilly, Virginia 20151
703-227-9600
czecher@bia.com

President Michael Schwab
Big Sky Partners, LLC
369 Broadway
Suite 301
San Francisco, California 94133
415-402-0459
michael@bigskyvc.com

General Manager Marc Faber
BIP Investment Partners S.A.
Rue des Coquelicots, 1
Luxembourg LU-1356
Luxembourg
352-2600-26-1
marc.faber@bip.lu

Director Finance and Control Jean Medernach
BIP Investment Partners S.A.
Rue des Coquelicots, 1
Luxembourg LU-1356
Luxembourg
352-2600-26-1
jean.medernach@bip.lu

VENTURE CAPITAL DIRECTORY

Senior Managing Director David S. Blitzer
Blackstone Group
40 Berkeley Square
London
W1J 5AL
United Kingdom
44-20-7451-4000
blitzer@blackstone.com

Senior Managing Director Chinh Chu
Blackstone Group
345 Park Avenue
New York, New York 10154
212-583-5000
chu@blackstone.com

Senior Managing Director Robert Friedman
Blackstone Group
345 Park Avenue
New York, New York 10154
212-583-5000

Senior Managing Director Lawrence Guffey
Blackstone Group
345 Park Avenue
New York, New York 10154
212-583-5000
guffey@blackstone.com

Senior Managing Director Prakash Melwani
Blackstone Group
345 Park Avenue
New York, New York 10154
212-583-5000

Senior Managing Director Neil Simpkins
Blackstone Group
345 Park Avenue
New York, New York 10154
212-583-5000
simpkins@blackstone.com

Senior Managing Director Kenneth Whitney
Blackstone Group
345 Park Avenue

VENTURE CAPITAL DIRECTORY

New York, New York 10154
212-583-5000
whitney@blackstone.com

Senior Managing Director James Quella
Blackstone Group
345 Park Avenue
New York, New York 10154
212-583-5000

Managing Director John McIlwraith
Blue Chip Venture Co.
1100 Chiquita Center
250 E. 5th Street
Cincinnati, Ohio 45202
513-723-2300
johnmci@bcvc.com

Managing Director John Wyant
Blue Chip Venture Co.
1100 Chiquita Center
250 E. 5th Street
Cincinnati, Ohio 45202
513-723-2300

Director Timothy Schigel
Blue Chip Venture Co.
1100 Chiquita Center
250 E. 5th Street
Cincinnati, Ohio 45202
513-723-2300
tim@bcvc.com

Director Gregory Taylor
Blue Chip Venture Co.
1100 Chiquita Center
250 E. 5th Street
Cincinnati, Ohio 45202
513-723-2300
greg@bcvc.com

Director Mark Wright
Blue Chip Venture Co.
1100 Chiquita Center
250 E. 5th Street
Cincinnati, Ohio 45202

VENTURE CAPITAL DIRECTORY

513-723-2300

Director Don Aquilano
Blue Chip Venture Co.
11611 North Meridian Street
Suite 310
Carmel, Indiana 46032
317-275-6800

Director Christopher McCleary
Blue Chip Venture Co.
1100 Chiquita Center
250 E. 5th Street
Cincinnati, Ohio 45202
513-723-2300

Associate Dov Rosenberg
Blue Chip Venture Co.
1100 Chiquita Center
250 E. 5th Street
Cincinnati, Ohio 45202
513-723-2300

Chairman and Managing Director Jonathan Blue
Blue Equity, LLC
333 East Main Street
Suite 200
Louisville, Kentucky 40202
502-589-8181
jblue@blueequity.com

Executive Vice President David Roth
Blue Equity, LLC
333 East Main Street
Suite 200
Louisville, Kentucky 40202
502-589-8181

COO Michael Principe
Blue Equity, LLC
333 East Main Street
Suite 200
Louisville, Kentucky 40202
502-589-8181

Senior Vice President Juan Reffreger

VENTURE CAPITAL DIRECTORY

Blue Equity, LLC
333 East Main Street
Suite 200
Louisville, Kentucky 40202
502-589-8181

General Partner Bo Baskin
Blue Sage Capital
114 W 7th Street
Suite 820
Austin, Texas 78701
512-536-1900
bo.baskin@bluesage.com

General Partner Peter Huff
Blue Sage Capital
114 W 7th Street
Suite 820
Austin, Texas 78701
512-536-1900
peter.huff@bluesage.com

General Partner Jim McBride
Blue Sage Capital
114 W 7th Street
Suite 820
Austin, Texas 78701
512-536-1900
jim.mcbride@bluesage.com

Director and Special Limited Partner Beverly Bendicksen
Blue Sage Capital
1155 University Boulevard, SE
Albuquerque, New Mexico 87106
505-843-4267
beverly.bendicksen@bluesage.com

Partner Jack Cardwell
Blue Sage Capital
114 W 7th Street
Suite 820
Austin, Texas 78701
512-536-1900
jack.cardwell@bluesage.com

President and CEO Steve Somerville

VENTURE CAPITAL DIRECTORY

BMO Capital Corporation
100 King Street West
First Canadian Place, 11th Floor
Toronto Ontario M5X 1A1
Canada
416-867-3208

Managing Director Eric Ehgoetz
BMO Capital Corporation
100 King Street West
First Canadian Place, 11th Floor
Toronto Ontario M5X 1A1
Canada
416-867-3208
eric.ehgoetz@bmo.com

Managing Director Claude Miron
BMO Capital Corporation
105 Saint-Jacques
3rd Floor
Montreal Quebec H2Y 1L6
Canada
514-877-1879
claude.miron@bmo.com

Managing Director Nadim Hirji
BMO Capital Corporation
350 - 7th Avenue SW
9th Floor, First Canadian Centre
Calgary Alberta T2P 3N9
Canada
403-234-1847
nadim.hirji@bmo.com

Managing Director Darren Yaworsky
BMO Capital Corporation
595 Burrard St.
6th Floor
Vancouver British Columbia V7X 1L7
Canada
604-668-1112
darren.yaworsky@bmo.com

bmp AG
Head of Investment Management Oliver Borrmann
Schlüterstrasse 38

VENTURE CAPITAL DIRECTORY

DE-10629 Berlin
Germany
49-30-20-305-0
oborrmann@bmp.com

bmp AG
Head of Portfolio Strategy Ralph Günther
Schlüterstrasse 38
DE-10629 Berlin
Germany
49-30-20-305-0
rguenther@bmp.com

bmp AG
CFO Andreas van Bon
Schlüterstrasse 38
DE-10629 Berlin
Germany
49-30-20-305-0
avanbon@bmp.com

Chairman Harald Ludwig
Bond Capital Partners (UK) Ltd.
21 Arlington Street
London
SW1A 1RN
United Kingdom
44-20-7491-6414
harald.ludwig@bondcapitalpartners.com

CEO Mark Opzoomer
Bond Capital Partners (UK) Ltd.
21 Arlington Street
London
SW1A 1RN
United Kingdom
44-20-7491-6414
mark.opzoomer@bondcapitalpartners.com

CFO Kin Huang
Bond Capital Partners (UK) Ltd.
21 Arlington Street
London
SW1A 1RN
United Kingdom
44-20-7491-6414

VENTURE CAPITAL DIRECTORY

kin.huang@bondcapitalpartners.com

Partner Barrie Moore
Bond Capital Partners (UK) Ltd.
21 Arlington Street
London
SW1A 1RN
United Kingdom
44-20-7491-6414
barrie.moore@bondcapitalpartners.com

Managing Director Roy Coppedge III
Boston Ventures Management, Inc.
One Federal Street
17th Floor
Boston, Massachusetts 2110
617-350-1500
rcoppedge@bvlp.com

Managing Director - Operating Partner Barry Baker
Boston Ventures Management, Inc.
One Federal Street
17th Floor
Boston, Massachusetts 2110
617-350-1500
bbaker@bvlp.com

Managing Director Anthony Bolland
Boston Ventures Management, Inc.
One Federal Street
17th Floor
Boston, Massachusetts 2110
617-350-1500
abolland@bvlp.com

Managing Director Andrew Davis
Boston Ventures Management, Inc.
One Federal Street
17th Floor
Boston, Massachusetts 2110
617-350-1500
adavis@bvlp.com

Managing Director Barbara Ginader
Boston Ventures Management, Inc.
One Federal Street

VENTURE CAPITAL DIRECTORY

17th Floor
Boston, Massachusetts 2110
617-350-1500
bginader@bvlp.com

Managing Director Elizabeth Granville-Smith
Boston Ventures Management, Inc.
One Federal Street
17th Floor
Boston, Massachusetts 2110
617-350-1500
egsmith@bvlp.com

Managing Director - Operating Partner Gerald Hobbs
Boston Ventures Management, Inc.
One Federal Street
17th Floor
Boston, Massachusetts 2110
617-350-1500
ghobbs@bvlp.com

Managing Director Vikrant Raina
Boston Ventures Management, Inc.
One Federal Street
17th Floor
Boston, Massachusetts 2110
617-350-1500
vraina@bvlp.com

Managing Director James Wilson
Boston Ventures Management, Inc.
One Federal Street
17th Floor
Boston, Massachusetts 2110
617-350-1500
jwilson@bvlp.com

Partner Joseph Casey
Boston Ventures Management, Inc.
One Federal Street
17th Floor
Boston, Massachusetts 2110
617-350-1500
jcasey@bvlp.com

Principal Louis Bertocci

VENTURE CAPITAL DIRECTORY

Boston Ventures Management, Inc.
One Federal Street
17th Floor
Boston, Massachusetts 2110
617-350-1500
lbertocci@bvlp.com

Principal Justin Harrison
Boston Ventures Management, Inc.
One Federal Street
17th Floor
Boston, Massachusetts 2110
617-350-1500
jharrison@bvlp.com

Principal Matthew Kinsey
Boston Ventures Management, Inc.
One Federal Street
17th Floor
Boston, Massachusetts 2110
617-350-1500
mkinsey@bvlp.com

Associate Marco Ferrari
Boston Ventures Management, Inc.
One Federal Street
17th Floor
Boston, Massachusetts 2110
617-350-1500
mferrari@bvlp.com

Associate Brian Weeks
Boston Ventures Management, Inc.
One Federal Street
17th Floor
Boston, Massachusetts 2110
617-350-1500
bweeks@bvlp.com

Managing Director Charles Ind
Bowmark Capital Ltd.
3 St James's Square
London
SW1Y 4JU
United Kingdom
44-20-7189-9000

VENTURE CAPITAL DIRECTORY

cind@bowmark.com

Managing Director Kevin Grassby
Bowmark Capital Ltd.
3 St James's Square
London
SW1Y 4JU
United Kingdom
44-20-7189-9000
kgrassby@bowmark.com

Director Duncan Calam
Bowmark Capital Ltd.
3 St James's Square
London
SW1Y 4JU
United Kingdom
44-20-7189-9000

Director Michael Simmonds
Bowmark Capital Ltd.
3 St James's Square
London
SW1Y 4JU
United Kingdom
44-20-7189-9000
msimmonds@bowmark.com

Director Niall McAteer
Bowmark Capital Ltd.
3 St James's Square
London
SW1Y 4JU
United Kingdom
44-20-7189-9000
nmcateer@bowmark.com

Director Mark Salter
Bowmark Capital Ltd.
3 St James's Square
London
SW1Y 4JU
United Kingdom
44-20-7189-9000

VENTURE CAPITAL DIRECTORY

Director Ron Pearson
Bowmark Capital Ltd.
3 St James's Square
London
SW1Y 4JU
United Kingdom
44-20-7189-9000
rpearson@bowmark.com

Partner Randall Fojtasek
Brazos Private Equity Partners, LLC
100 Crescent Court
Suite 1777
Dallas, Texas 75201
214-756-6500
rfojtasek@brazosinv.com

Partner Jeff Fronterhouse
Brazos Private Equity Partners, LLC
100 Crescent Court
Suite 1777
Dallas, Texas 75201
214-756-6500
jfronterhouse@brazosinv.com

Partner Patrick McGee
Brazos Private Equity Partners, LLC
100 Crescent Court
Suite 1777
Dallas, Texas 75201
214-756-6500
pmcgee@brazosinv.com

Partner and General Counsel Michael Salim
Brazos Private Equity Partners, LLC
100 Crescent Court
Suite 1777
Dallas, Texas 75201
214-756-6500
msalim@brazosinv.com

Vice President Glenn Askew III
Brazos Private Equity Partners, LLC
100 Crescent Court
Suite 1777
Dallas, Texas 75201

VENTURE CAPITAL DIRECTORY

214-756-6500
gaskew@brazosinv.com

Vice President David Mann
Brazos Private Equity Partners, LLC
100 Crescent Court
Suite 1777
Dallas, Texas 75201
214-756-6500
dmann@brazosinv.com

Senior Associate Lucas Cutler
Brazos Private Equity Partners, LLC
100 Crescent Court
Suite 1777
Dallas, Texas 75201
214-756-6500
lcutler@brazosinv.com

Senior Associate Megan Taylor
Brazos Private Equity Partners, LLC
100 Crescent Court
Suite 1777
Dallas, Texas 75201
214-756-6500
mtaylor@brazosinv.com

Associate F. Russell Beard Jr.
Brazos Private Equity Partners, LLC
100 Crescent Court
Suite 1777
Dallas, Texas 75201
214-756-6500
rbeard@brazosinv.com

Analyst Charles von Faber-Castell
Brazos Private Equity Partners, LLC
100 Crescent Court
Suite 1777
Dallas, Texas 75201
214-756-6500
cfaber-castell@brazosinv.com

General Partner William Barnum Jr.
Brentwood Associates
11150 Santa Monica Blvd.

VENTURE CAPITAL DIRECTORY

Suite 1200
Los Angeles, California 90025
310-477-6611
bbarnum@brentwood.com

General Partner Edward McCall
Brentwood Associates
11150 Santa Monica Blvd.
Suite 1200
Los Angeles, California 90025
310-477-6611
emccall@brentwood.com

General Partner Anthony Choe
Brentwood Associates
11150 Santa Monica Blvd.
Suite 1200
Los Angeles, California 90025
310-477-6611
achoe@brentwood.com

General Partner Roger Goddu
Brentwood Associates
11150 Santa Monica Blvd.
Suite 1200
Los Angeles, California 90025
310-477-6611
rgoddu@brentwood.com

Principal Rahul Aggarwal
Brentwood Associates
11150 Santa Monica Blvd.
Suite 1200
Los Angeles, California 90025
310-477-6611

Principal Eric Reiter
Brentwood Associates
11150 Santa Monica Blvd.
Suite 1200
Los Angeles, California 90025
310-477-6611

Principal Steven Moore
Brentwood Associates
11150 Santa Monica Blvd.

VENTURE CAPITAL DIRECTORY

Suite 1200
Los Angeles, California 90025
310-477-6611

Operating Principal Randolph Brown
Brentwood Associates
11150 Santa Monica Blvd.
Suite 1200
Los Angeles, California 90025
310-477-6611

Senior Associate Toros Yeremyan
Brentwood Associates
11150 Santa Monica Blvd.
Suite 1200
Los Angeles, California 90025
310-477-6611

Senior Associate Eugene Yea
Brentwood Associates
11150 Santa Monica Blvd.
Suite 1200
Los Angeles, California 90025
310-477-6611

Chairman David Shaw
Bridgepoint Capital Ltd.
30 Warwick Street
London
W1B 5AL
United Kingdom
44-20-7374-3500
david.shaw@bridgepoint.eu

Managing Partner William Jackson
Bridgepoint Capital Ltd.
30 Warwick Street
London
W1B 5AL
United Kingdom
44-20-7374-3500
william.jackson@bridgepoint.eu

Partner Kevin Reynolds
Bridgepoint Capital Ltd.
30 Warwick Street

VENTURE CAPITAL DIRECTORY

London
W1B 5AL
United Kingdom
44-20-7374-3500
kevin.reynolds@bridgepoint.eu

Partner Alan Lewis
Bridgepoint Capital Ltd.
30 Warwick Street
London
W1B 5AL
United Kingdom
44-20-7374-3500
alan.lewis@bridgepoint.eu

Partner Vince Gwilliam
Bridgepoint Capital Ltd.
30 Warwick Street
London
W1B 5AL
United Kingdom
44-20-7374-3500
vince.gwilliam@bridgepoint.eu

Partner Michael Black
Bridgepoint Capital Ltd.
30 Warwick Street
London
W1B 5AL
United Kingdom
44-20-7374-3500
michael.black@bridgepoint.eu

Partner Michael Davy
Bridgepoint Capital Ltd.
30 Warwick Street
London
W1B 5AL
United Kingdom
44-20-7374-3500
michael.davy@bridgepoint.eu

Director Martin Dunn
Bridgepoint Capital Ltd.
30 Warwick Street
London

VENTURE CAPITAL DIRECTORY

W1B 5AL
United Kingdom
44-20-7374-3500
martin.dunn@bridgepoint.eu

Partner Rob Moores
Bridgepoint Capital Ltd.
30 Warwick Street
London
W1B 5AL
United Kingdom
44-20-7374-3500
rob.moores@bridgepoint.eu

Director Michael Walton
Bridgepoint Capital Ltd.
30 Warwick Street
London
W1B 5AL
United Kingdom
44-20-7374-3500
michael.walton@bridgepoint.eu

Partner Guy Weldon
Bridgepoint Capital Ltd.
30 Warwick Street
London
W1B 5AL
United Kingdom
44-20-7374-3500
guy.weldon@bridgepoint.eu

Director Alan Payne
Bridgepoint Capital Ltd.
30 Warwick Street
London
W1B 5AL
United Kingdom
44-20-7374-3500
alan.payne@bridgepoint.eu

Director Ursula Korpert
Bridgepoint Capital Ltd.
30 Warwick Street
London
W1B 5AL

VENTURE CAPITAL DIRECTORY

United Kingdom
44-20-7374-3500
ursula.korpert@bridgepoint.eu

Partner Benoît Bassi
Bridgepoint Capital SAS
37-39 rue de la Bienfaisance
FR-75008 Paris
France
33-1-4429-2100
benoit.bassi@bridgepoint.eu

Partner Valérie Texier
Bridgepoint Capital SAS
37-39 rue de la Bienfaisance
FR-75008 Paris
France
33-1-4429-2100
valerie.texier@bridgepoint.eu

Investment Director Vincent Briançon
Bridgepoint Capital SAS
37-39 rue de la Bienfaisance
FR-75008 Paris
France
33-1-4429-2100
vincent.briancon@bridgepoint.eu

Investment Director Pierre Colasson
Bridgepoint Capital SAS
37-39 rue de la Bienfaisance
FR-75008 Paris
France
33-1-4429-2100
pierre.colasson@bridgepoint.eu

Executive Hoang Kim Nguyen
Bridgepoint Capital SAS
37-39 rue de la Bienfaisance
FR-75008 Paris
France
33-1-4429-2100
kim.nguyen@bridgepoint.eu

Executive Vincent-Gaël Baudet
Bridgepoint Capital SAS

VENTURE CAPITAL DIRECTORY

37-39 rue de la Bienfaisance
FR-75008 Paris
France
33-1-4429-2100
vincent-gael.baudet@bridgepoint.eu

Partner Andrew Clapp
Brook Venture Partners
301 Edgewater Place
4th Floor
Wakefield, Massachusetts 1880
781-295-4000
andy4@brookventure.com

Partner Frederic Morris
Brook Venture Partners
301 Edgewater Place
4th Floor
Wakefield, Massachusetts 1880
781-295-4000
fmorris@brookventure.com

Partner Edward Williams III
Brook Venture Partners
301 Edgewater Place
4th Floor
Wakefield, Massachusetts 1880
781-295-4000
ewilliams@brookventure.com

Partner Walter Beinecke
Brook Venture Partners
301 Edgewater Place
4th Floor
Wakefield, Massachusetts 1880
781-295-4000
wbeinecke@brookventure.com

Associate Jeffrey Emig
Brook Venture Partners
301 Edgewater Place
4th Floor
Wakefield, Massachusetts 1880
781-295-4000
jemig@brookventure.com

VENTURE CAPITAL DIRECTORY

Analyst Nicholas Bouquet
Brook Venture Partners
301 Edgewater Place
4th Floor
Wakefield, Massachusetts 1880
781-295-4000
nbouquet@brookventure.com

Chairman Peter Brooke
Brooke Private Equity Advisors
114 State Street
6th Floor
Boston, Massachusetts 2109
617-227-3160
pbrooke@brookepea.com

Partner John Brooke
Brooke Private Equity Advisors
114 State Street
6th Floor
Boston, Massachusetts 2109
617-227-3160
jbrooke@brookepea.com

Partner H.J. von der Goltz
Brooke Private Equity Advisors
114 State Street
6th Floor
Boston, Massachusetts 2109
617-227-3160
jgoltz@brookepea.com

Partner Charles Bridge
Brooke Private Equity Advisors
114 State Street
6th Floor
Boston, Massachusetts 2109
617-227-3160
cbridge@brookepea.com

Partner Chris Austen
Brooke Private Equity Advisors
114 State Street
6th Floor
Boston, Massachusetts 2109
617-227-3160

VENTURE CAPITAL DIRECTORY

chubbard@brookepea.com

Partner Lawrence Tucker
Brown Brothers Harriman & Co.
140 Broadway
New York, New York 10005-1101
212-493-7972
lawrence.tucker@bbh.com

Partner T. Michael Long
Brown Brothers Harriman & Co.
140 Broadway
New York, New York 10005-1101
212-493-7972
michael.long@bbh.com

Managing Director Walter Grist
Brown Brothers Harriman & Co.
140 Broadway
New York, New York 10005-1101
212-493-7972
walter.grist@bbh.com

Senior Vice President and CFO Charles Schreiber
Brown Brothers Harriman & Co.
140 Broadway
New York, New York 10005-1101
212-493-7972
charles.schreiber@bbh.com

Managing Director Jeffrey Meskin
Brown Brothers Harriman & Co.
140 Broadway
New York, New York 10005-1101
212-493-7972
jeffrey.meskin@bbh.com

Managing Partner Shedde Pramod D.
BTS Investment Advisors Private Ltd.,
704 / 705 Balarama,
Bandra Kurla Complex, Bandra East,
Mumbai - 400 051,
India
91-22-5697-8292
pshedde@btsadvisors.com

Managing Partner Srinivas K.

VENTURE CAPITAL DIRECTORY

BTS Investment Advisors Private Ltd.,
704 / 705 Balarama,
Bandra Kurla Complex, Bandra East,
Mumbai - 400 051,
India
91-22-5697-8292
srinivas@btsadvisors.com

Vice President Gupta Suneet
BTS Investment Advisors Private Ltd.,
704 / 705 Balarama,
Bandra Kurla Complex, Bandra East,
Mumbai - 400 051,
India
91-22-5697-8292
suneet@btsadvisors.com

Vice President Dighe Bharat
BTS Investment Advisors Private Ltd.,
704 / 705 Balarama,
Bandra Kurla Complex, Bandra East,
Mumbai - 400 051,
India
91-22-5697-8292
bharat@btsadvisors.com

Assistant Vice President Lacerda Kenneth
BTS Investment Advisors Private Ltd.,
704 / 705 Balarama,
Bandra Kurla Complex, Bandra East,
Mumbai - 400 051,
India
91-22-5697-8292
kenneth@btsadvisors.com

CFO Sharma Rajiv
BTS Investment Advisors Private Ltd.,
704 / 705 Balarama,
Bandra Kurla Complex, Bandra East,
Mumbai - 400 051,
India
91-22-5697-8292
rajiv@btsadvisors.com

Vice President Baliga Subhash
BTS Investment Advisors Private Ltd.,

VENTURE CAPITAL DIRECTORY

704 / 705 Balarama,
Bandra Kurla Complex, Bandra East,
Mumbai - 400 051,
India
91-22-5697-8292
subhash@btsadvisors.com

Associate Vice President Pullabhatla Rakesh
BTS Investment Advisors Private Ltd.,
704 / 705 Balarama,
Bandra Kurla Complex, Bandra East,
Mumbai - 400 051,
India
91-22-5697-8292
rakesh@btsadvisors.com

Associate Vice President Varghese Shaji
BTS Investment Advisors Private Ltd.,
704 / 705 Balarama,
Bandra Kurla Complex, Bandra East,
Mumbai - 400 051,
India
91-22-5697-8292
shaji@btsadvisors.com

CEO Mohd As'ad Sidon
BTVC Bhd.
14th Floor Menara PSCI
Jalan Sultan Ahmad Shah
Pulau Pinang 10050
Malaysia
60-4-227-4297
asadsidon@btvc.com.my

Investment Manager Shaik Othman Hussain
BTVC Bhd.
14th Floor Menara PSCI
Jalan Sultan Ahmad Shah
Pulau Pinang 10050
Malaysia
60-4-227-4297
shaik@btvc.com.my

Investment Analyst Norliza Jaafar
BTVC Bhd.
14th Floor Menara PSCI

VENTURE CAPITAL DIRECTORY

Jalan Sultan Ahmad Shah
Pulau Pinang 10050
Malaysia
60-4-227-4297
liza@btvc.com.my

BV Capital
Partner, Europe Wolfgang Rose
Grosse Elbstrasse 145D
DE-22767 Hamburg
Germany
49-40-8222-555-0
wolfgang@bvcapital.com

BV Capital
CFO, Europe Maren Eckloff-Boehme
Grosse Elbstrasse 145D
DE-22767 Hamburg
Germany
49-40-8222-555-0
meckloff@bvcapital.com

BV Capital
Principal, Europe Christian Leybold
Grosse Elbstrasse 145D
DE-22767 Hamburg
Germany
49-40-8222-555-0
christian@bvcapital.com

Partner, US Jan Henric Buettner
BV Capital
600 Montgomery Street
43rd Floor
San Francisco, California 94111
415-869-5200
jan@bvcapital.com

Partner, US Mathias Schilling
BV Capital
600 Montgomery Street
43rd Floor
San Francisco, California 94111
415-869-5200
mathias@bvcapital.com

VENTURE CAPITAL DIRECTORY

Partner, US Thomas Gieselmann
BV Capital
600 Montgomery Street
43rd Floor
San Francisco, California 94111
415-869-5200
tom@bvcapital.com

Partner, US Andreas von Blottnitz
BV Capital
600 Montgomery Street
43rd Floor
San Francisco, California 94111
415-869-5200
ablottnitz@bvcapital.com

Managing Director and Head of France Cyrille Chevrillon
Candover Investments plc
21-25 rue Balzac
FR-75008 Paris
France
33-1-5836-4350
c.chevrillon@candover.com

Candover Investments plc
Director and Head of Germany Jens Tonn
Steinstrasse 11
DE-40212 Düsseldorf
Germany
49-211-617050-0
j.tonn@candover.com

Director and Head of Italy Aldo Maccari
Candover Investments plc
Galleria San Carlo 6
IT-20122 Milan
Italy
39-2-7631-6002
a.maccari@candover.com

Director Javier Abad
Candover Investments plc
Ayala 11
ES-28001 Madrid
Spain
34-91-426-3851

VENTURE CAPITAL DIRECTORY

j.abad@candover.com

Managing Director Colin J. Buffin
Candover Investments plc
20 Old Bailey
London
EC4M 7LN
United Kingdom
44-20-7489-9848
c.buffin@candover.com

Managing Director Marek S. Gumienny
Candover Investments plc
20 Old Bailey
London
EC4M 7LN
United Kingdom
44-20-7489-9848
m.gumienny@candover.com

Managing Director John Arney
Candover Investments plc
20 Old Bailey
London
EC4M 7LN
United Kingdom
44-20-7489-9848
j.arney@candover.com

Director Julian Delano
Candover Investments plc
20 Old Bailey
London
EC4M 7LN
United Kingdom
44-20-7489-9848
j.delano@candover.com

Managing Director Ian Gray
Candover Investments plc
20 Old Bailey
London
EC4M 7LN
United Kingdom
44-20-7489-9848
i.gray@candover.com

VENTURE CAPITAL DIRECTORY

Managing Director Charlie Green
Candover Investments plc
20 Old Bailey
London
EC4M 7LN
United Kingdom
44-20-7489-9848
c.green@candover.com

Managing Director Simon Leefe
Candover Investments plc
20 Old Bailey
London
EC4M 7LN
United Kingdom
44-20-7489-9848
s.leefe@candover.com

Director Brian Mercer
Candover Investments plc
20 Old Bailey
London
EC4M 7LN
United Kingdom
44-20-7489-9848
b.mercer@candover.com

CAPEXIT Beteiligungsmanagement AG
Partner
Johannes Krahwinkler
Rathausstrasse 19/1/Top 53
AT-1010 Vienna
Austria
43-1-402-3752-0
j.krahwinkler@capexit.at

CAPEXIT Beteiligungsmanagement AG
Partner
Christian Kaltenegger
Rathausstrasse 19/1/Top 53
AT-1010 Vienna
Austria
43-1-402-3752-0
c.kaltenegger@capexit.at

VENTURE CAPITAL DIRECTORY

CAPEXIT Beteiligungsmanagement AG
Partner
Siegfried Mörz
Rathausstrasse 19/1/Top 53
AT-1010 Vienna
Austria
43-1-402-3752-0
s.moerz@capexit.at

CAPEXIT Beteiligungsmanagement AG
Business Analyst
Ernst Ungersbäck
Rathausstrasse 19/1/Top 53
AT-1010 Vienna
Austria
43-1-402-3752-0
e.ungersbaeck@capexit.at

President and Chairman William Thomas
Capital Southwest Corporation
12900 Preston Road
Suite 700
Dallas, Texas 75230
972-233-8242

Senior Vice President William Ashbaugh
Capital Southwest Corporation
12900 Preston Road
Suite 700
Dallas, Texas 75230
972-233-8242
bashbaugh@capitalsouthwest.com

Vice President Jeffrey Peterson
Capital Southwest Corporation
12900 Preston Road
Suite 700
Dallas, Texas 75230
972-233-8242
peterson@capitalsouthwest.com

Secretary-Treasurer Susan Hodgson
Capital Southwest Corporation
12900 Preston Road
Suite 700
Dallas, Texas 75230

VENTURE CAPITAL DIRECTORY

972-233-8242
skhodgson@capitalsouthwest.com

Investment Associate William Thomas III
Capital Southwest Corporation
12900 Preston Road
Suite 700
Dallas, Texas 75230
972-233-8242
will.thomas@capitalsouthwest.com

Chairman R. Steven Hicks
Capstar Partners, LLC
600 Congress Ave.
Suite 1400
Austin, Texas 78701
512-340-7800
shicks@capstarpartners.com

Partner John Cullen
Capstar Partners, LLC
600 Congress Ave.
Suite 1400
Austin, Texas 78701
512-340-7800
jcullen@capstarpartners.com

Partner Paul Stone
Capstar Partners, LLC
600 Congress Ave.
Suite 1400
Austin, Texas 78701
512-340-7800
pstone@capstarpartners.com

Principal Benjamin Hanson
Capstar Partners, LLC
600 Congress Ave.
Suite 1400
Austin, Texas 78701
512-340-7800
bhanson@capstarpartners.com

Founding Partner and Managing Director William Conway Jr.
Carlyle Group
1001 Pennsylvania Ave, NW

VENTURE CAPITAL DIRECTORY

Washington, District of Columbia 20004
202-729-5626
Founding Partner and Managing Director Daniel D'Aniello
Carlyle Group
1001 Pennsylvania Ave, NW
Washington, District of Columbia 20004
202-729-5626

Co-Founder and Managing Director David Rubenstein
Carlyle Group
1001 Pennsylvania Ave, NW
Washington, District of Columbia 20004
202-729-5626

Managing Partner Brian Knez
Castanea Partners
Three Newton Executive Park
Suite 304
Newton, Massachusetts 2462
617-630-2400
bknez@castaneapartners.com

Managing Partner Robert Smith
Castanea Partners
Three Newton Executive Park
Suite 304
Newton, Massachusetts 2462
617-630-2400
rsmith@castaneapartners.com

Partner Paul Gibbons
Castanea Partners
Three Newton Executive Park
Suite 304
Newton, Massachusetts 2462
617-630-2400
pgibbons@castaneapartners.com

Partner Steven Berg
Castanea Partners
Three Newton Executive Park
Suite 304
Newton, Massachusetts 2462
617-630-2400
sberg@castaneapartners.com

VENTURE CAPITAL DIRECTORY

Operating Partner David Flaschen
Castanea Partners
Three Newton Executive Park
Suite 304
Newton, Massachusetts 2462
617-630-2400
dflaschen@castaneapartners.com

Principal Troy Stanfield
Castanea Partners
Three Newton Executive Park
Suite 304
Newton, Massachusetts 2462
617-630-2400
tstanfield@castaneapartners.com

CFO Colleen Love
Castanea Partners
Three Newton Executive Park
Suite 304
Newton, Massachusetts 2462
617-630-2400
clove@castaneapartners.com

Principal Rick Herrman
Catalyst Group, Inc.
Two Riverway
Suite 1710
Houston, Texas 77056
713-623-8133
herrman@thecatalystgroup.net

Principal Ron Nixon
Catalyst Group, Inc.
Two Riverway
Suite 1710
Houston, Texas 77056
713-623-8133
nixon@thecatalystgroup.net

Principal Roger Linn
Catalyst Group, Inc.
7820 Hanger Cutoff Road
Fort Worth, Texas 76135
817-237-2200
linn@thecatalystgroup.net

VENTURE CAPITAL DIRECTORY

Principal Steve Gillioz
Catalyst Group, Inc.
Two Riverway
Suite 1710
Houston, Texas 77056
713-623-8133
gillioz@thecatalystgroup.net

Principal Walter Weathers
Catalyst Group, Inc.
Two Riverway
Suite 1710
Houston, Texas 77056
713-623-8133
wweathers@thecatalystgroup.net

Managing Partner Brian Rich
Catalyst Investors, L.P.
711 Fifth Avenue
Suite 402
New York, New York 10022
212-863-4848
brian@catalystinvestors.com

General Partner Christopher Shipman
Catalyst Investors, L.P.
711 Fifth Avenue
Suite 402
New York, New York 10022
212-863-4848
chris@catalystinvestors.com

General Partner Ryan McNally
Catalyst Investors, L.P.
711 Fifth Avenue
Suite 402
New York, New York 10022
212-863-4848
ryan@catalystinvestors.com

Partner Tyler Newton
Catalyst Investors, L.P.
711 Fifth Avenue
Suite 402
New York, New York 10022
212-863-4848

VENTURE CAPITAL DIRECTORY

tyler@catalystinvestors.com

Principal Todd Clap
Catalyst Investors, L.P.
711 Fifth Avenue
Suite 402
New York, New York 10022
212-863-4848
todd@catalystinvestors.com

Principal Rick Herrman
Catalyst/Hall Growth Capital
Two Riverway
Suite 1710
Houston, Texas 77056
713-623-8133
rherrman@catalysthall.com

Principal Stephen Gillioz
Catalyst/Hall Growth Capital
Two Riverway
Suite 1710
Houston, Texas 77056
713-623-8133
sgillioz@catalysthall.com

Principal Roger Linn
Catalyst/Hall Growth Capital
Two Riverway
Suite 1710
Houston, Texas 77056
713-623-8133
rlinn@catalysthall.com

Principal Ron Nixon
Catalyst/Hall Growth Capital
Two Riverway
Suite 1710
Houston, Texas 77056
713-623-8133
rnixon@catalysthall.com

Principal John Kobza
Catalyst/Hall Growth Capital
One Westminster Place
Suite 108

VENTURE CAPITAL DIRECTORY

Lake Forest, Illinois 60045
847-295-4214
jkobza@catalysthall.com
Principal David Holsted
Catalyst/Hall Growth Capital
9225 Lake Hefner Parkway
Suite 200
Oklahoma City, Oklahoma 73120
405-231-2400
dholsted@catalysthall.com

Principal Walter Weathers
Catalyst/Hall Growth Capital
Two Riverway
Suite 1710
Houston, Texas 77056
713-623-8133
wweathers@catalysthall.com

Chairman and Managing Partner Frederick Iseman
Caxton-Iseman Capital, Inc.
500 Park Avenue
New York, New York 10022
212-752-1850

Managing Director Robert Ferris
Caxton-Iseman Capital, Inc.
500 Park Avenue
New York, New York 10022
212-752-1850

Managing Director Steven Lefkowitz
Caxton-Iseman Capital, Inc.
500 Park Avenue
New York, New York 10022
212-752-1850
slefkowitz@caxton-iseman.com

Principal Timothy Hall
Caxton-Iseman Capital, Inc.
500 Park Avenue
New York, New York 10022
212-752-1850

Principal Joost Thesseling
Caxton-Iseman Capital, Inc.

VENTURE CAPITAL DIRECTORY

500 Park Avenue
New York, New York 10022
212-752-1850
jthesseling@caxton-iseman.com

Vice President David Brady
Caxton-Iseman Capital, Inc.
500 Park Avenue
New York, New York 10022
212-752-1850

Vice President Tom Ritchie
Caxton-Iseman Capital, Inc.
500 Park Avenue
New York, New York 10022
212-752-1850
tritchie@caxton-iseman.com

Vice President Ankur Vora
Caxton-Iseman Capital, Inc.
500 Park Avenue
New York, New York 10022
212-752-1850

Chairman Jeffrey Walker
CCMP Capital Advisors, LLC
245 Park Avenue
16th Floor
New York, New York 10167-2403
212-600-9600
jeffrey.walker@ccmpcapital.com

President and CEO Stephen Murray
CCMP Capital Advisors, LLC
245 Park Avenue
16th Floor
New York, New York 10167-2403
212-600-9600
stephen.murray@ccmpcapital.com

Managing Director Christopher Behrens
CCMP Capital Advisors, LLC
245 Park Avenue
16th Floor
New York, New York 10167-2403
212-600-9600

VENTURE CAPITAL DIRECTORY

christopher.behrens@ccmpcapital.com

Managing Director Michael Hannon
CCMP Capital Advisors, LLC
245 Park Avenue
16th Floor
New York, New York 10167-2403
212-600-9600
michael.hannon@ccmpcapital.com

Managing Director Jonathan Lynch
CCMP Capital Advisors, LLC
245 Park Avenue
16th Floor
New York, New York 10167-2403
212-600-9600
jonathan.lynch@ccmpcapital.com

Managing Director Timothy Walsh
CCMP Capital Advisors, LLC
245 Park Avenue
16th Floor
New York, New York 10167-2403
212-600-9600
timothy.walsh@ccmpcapital.com

Managing Director Richard Waters
CCMP Capital Advisors, LLC
245 Park Avenue
16th Floor
New York, New York 10167-2403
212-600-9600
richards.waters@ccmpcapital.com

Senior Member Stephen Welton
CCMP Capital Advisors (UK), LLP
Almack House
28 King Street
London
SW1Y 6XA
United Kingdom
44-20-7389-9100
stephen.welton@ccmpcapital.com

VENTURE CAPITAL DIRECTORY

Senior Member Thomas Walker
CCMP Capital Advisors (UK), LLP
Almack House
28 King Street
London
SW1Y 6XA
United Kingdom
44-20-7389-9100

Principal Raf Goovaerts
CCMP Capital Advisors (UK), LLP
Almack House
28 King Street
London
SW1Y 6XA
United Kingdom
44-20-7389-9100

Principal Heinz Holsten
CCMP Capital Advisors (UK), LLP
Almack House
28 King Street
London
SW1Y 6XA
United Kingdom
44-20-7389-9100

Principal Umur Hursever
CCMP Capital Advisors (UK), LLP
Almack House
28 King Street
London
SW1Y 6XA
United Kingdom
44-20-7389-9100

Co-Founder Scott Anderson
Cedar Grove Investments
1000 Second Avenue
#1200
Seattle, Washington 98104
206-332-1215
sanderson@cedargroveinv.com

Co-Founder Scot Jarvis
Cedar Grove Investments

VENTURE CAPITAL DIRECTORY

1000 Second Avenue
#1200
Seattle, Washington 98104
206-332-1215
sjarvis@cedargroveinv.com

Partner Mark Callaghan
Cedar Grove Investments
1000 Second Avenue
#1200
Seattle, Washington 98104
206-332-1215
mcallaghan@cedargroveinv.com

Partner Chris Birkeland
Cedar Grove Investments
1000 Second Avenue
#1200
Seattle, Washington 98104
206-332-1215
cbirkeland@cedargroveinv.com

Partner Bill Heston
Cedar Grove Investments
1000 Second Avenue
#1200
Seattle, Washington 98104
206-332-1215
bheston@cedargroveinv.com

Partner Tom Hughes
Cedar Grove Investments
1000 Second Avenue
#1200
Seattle, Washington 98104
206-332-1215
thughes@cedargroveinv.com

Managing Director Jeffrey Schutz
Centennial Ventures
1428 Fifteenth Street
Denver, Colorado 80202
303-405-7500
jschutz@centennial.com

VENTURE CAPITAL DIRECTORY

Managing Director Steve Halstedt
Centennial Ventures
1428 Fifteenth Street
Denver, Colorado 80202
303-405-7500
shalstedt@centennial.com

Managing Director Duncan Butler
Centennial Ventures
1428 Fifteenth Street
Denver, Colorado 80202
303-405-7500
dbutler@centennial.com

Managing Director David Hull
Centennial Ventures
1330 Post Oak Blvd.
Suite 1525
Houston, Texas 77056
713-627-9200
dhull@centennial.com

Managing Director Rand Lewis
Centennial Ventures
1428 Fifteenth Street
Denver, Colorado 80202
303-405-7500
rand@centennial.com

Managing Director Neel Sarkar
Centennial Ventures
600 Congress Avenue
Suite 200
Austin, Texas 78701
512-505-4500
neel@centennial.com

Senior Associate Ben Moss
Centennial Ventures
600 Congress Avenue
Suite 200
Austin, Texas 78701
512-505-4500
bmoss@centennial.com

Senior Associate Andy Rourke

VENTURE CAPITAL DIRECTORY

Centennial Ventures
1428 Fifteenth Street
Denver, Colorado 80202
303-405-7500

Senior Associate Jason Booma
Centennial Ventures
1428 Fifteenth Street
Denver, Colorado 80202
303-405-7500

CFO Bob Keppler
Centennial Ventures
1428 Fifteenth Street
Denver, Colorado 80202
303-405-7500

Chairman Lester Pollack
Centre Partners Management, LLC
30 Rockefeller Plaza
50th Floor
New York, New York 10020
212-332-5800
lester.pollack@centrepartners.com

Managing Partner David Jaffe
Centre Partners Management, LLC
30 Rockefeller Plaza
50th Floor
New York, New York 10020
212-332-5800
david.jaffe@centrepartners.com

Managing Partner Bruce Pollack
Centre Partners Management, LLC
30 Rockefeller Plaza
50th Floor
New York, New York 10020
212-332-5800
bruce.pollack@centrepartners.com

Senior Partner Robert Bergmann
Centre Partners Management, LLC
11726 San Vicente Blvd.
Suite 450
Los Angeles, California 90049

VENTURE CAPITAL DIRECTORY

310-207-9170
robert.bergmann@centrepartners.com

Joseph Ciechanover
Challenge Fund - Etgar L.P.
20 Lincoln Street
Rubenstein House, 20th Floor
Tel Aviv 67134
Israel
972-3-562-8555
joseph@challenge.co.il

Yossi Vinitski
Challenge Fund - Etgar L.P.
20 Lincoln Street
Rubenstein House, 20th Floor
Tel Aviv 67134
Israel
972-3-562-8555
vini@challenge.co.il

Erez Lorber
Challenge Fund - Etgar L.P.
20 Lincoln Street
Rubenstein House, 20th Floor
Tel Aviv 67134
Israel
972-3-562-8555
erez@challenge.co.il

Tamar Ciehanover
Challenge Fund - Etgar L.P.
20 Lincoln Street
Rubenstein House, 20th Floor
Tel Aviv 67134
Israel
972-3-562-8555
tamarc@challenge.co.il

Omri Rothman
Challenge Fund - Etgar L.P.
20 Lincoln Street
Rubenstein House, 20th Floor
Tel Aviv 67134
Israel
972-3-562-8555

VENTURE CAPITAL DIRECTORY

omri@challenge.co.il

Yossi Pastel
Challenge Fund - Etgar L.P.
20 Lincoln Street
Rubenstein House, 20th Floor
Tel Aviv 67134
Israel
972-3-562-8555
yp@challenge.co.il

CHAMP Ventures Pty Ltd.
Su-Ming Wong
Level 4, Customs House
31 Alfred Street
Sydney New South Wales 2000
Australia
61-2-8248-8822

CHAMP Ventures Pty Ltd.
Andrew Savage
Level 4, Customs House
31 Alfred Street
Sydney New South Wales 2000
Australia
61-2-8248-8822

CHAMP Ventures Pty Ltd.
Stuart Wardman-Browne
Level 4, Customs House
31 Alfred Street
Sydney New South Wales 2000
Australia
61-2-8248-8822

CHAMP Ventures Pty Ltd.
James Wentworth
Level 4, Customs House
31 Alfred Street
Sydney New South Wales 2000
Australia
61-2-8248-8822

CHAMP Ventures Pty Ltd.
Jonathan Kelly

VENTURE CAPITAL DIRECTORY

Level 4, Customs House
31 Alfred Street
Sydney New South Wales 2000
Australia
61-2-8248-8822
jkelly@champventures.com

CHAMP Ventures Pty Ltd.
Gareth Banks
Level 4, Customs House
31 Alfred Street
Sydney New South Wales 2000
Australia
61-2-8248-8822

CHAMP Ventures Pty Ltd.
Barry Zuckerman
Level 4, Customs House
31 Alfred Street
Sydney New South Wales 2000
Australia
61-2-8248-8822

General Partner Bruce Sachs
Charles River Ventures
1000 Winter Street
Waltham, Massachusetts 2451
781-768-6000
mgcurcio@crv.com

General Partner Ted Dintersmith
Charles River Ventures
1000 Winter Street
Waltham, Massachusetts 2451
781-768-6000
afandel@crv.com

General Partner Chris Baldwin
Charles River Ventures
1000 Winter Street
Waltham, Massachusetts 2451
781-768-6000
couellette@crv.com

VENTURE CAPITAL DIRECTORY

General Partner Bill Tai
Charles River Ventures
2800 Sand Hill Road
Suite 150
Menlo Park, California 94025
650-687-5600
tplumer@crv.com

General Partner Izhar Armony
Charles River Ventures
1000 Winter Street
Waltham, Massachusetts 2451
781-768-6000
anne-marie@crv.com

General Partner Rick Burnes
Charles River Ventures
1000 Winter Street
Waltham, Massachusetts 2451
781-768-6000
afandel@crv.com

General Partner Mike Zak
Charles River Ventures
1000 Winter Street
Waltham, Massachusetts 2451
781-768-6000
afandel@crv.com

General Partner Austin Westerling
Charles River Ventures
1000 Winter Street
Waltham, Massachusetts 2451
781-768-6000
anne-marie@crv.com

General Partner George Zachary
Charles River Ventures
2800 Sand Hill Road
Suite 150
Menlo Park, California 94025
650-687-5600
kmorioka@crv.com

VENTURE CAPITAL DIRECTORY

General Counsel Sarah Reed
Charles River Ventures
1000 Winter Street
Waltham, Massachusetts 2451
781-768-6000
sreed@crv.com

CFO Joe Monaco
Charles River Ventures
1000 Winter Street
Waltham, Massachusetts 2451
781-768-6000
jmonaco@crv.com

General Partner Saar Gur
Charles River Ventures
2800 Sand Hill Road
Suite 150
Menlo Park, California 94025
650-687-5600
sgur@crv.com

General Partner Susan Wu
Charles River Ventures
1000 Winter Street
Waltham, Massachusetts 2451
781-768-6000
swu@crv.com

Managing Director and CEO Michael Eisenson
Charlesbank Capital Partners, LLC
200 Clarendon Street
54th Floor
Boston, Massachusetts 2116
617-619-5400
meisenson@charlesbank.com

Managing Director and COO Michael Thonis
Charlesbank Capital Partners, LLC
200 Clarendon Street
54th Floor
Boston, Massachusetts 2116
617-619-5400
mthonis@charlesbank.com

Managing Director Tim Palmer

VENTURE CAPITAL DIRECTORY

Charlesbank Capital Partners, LLC
200 Clarendon Street
54th Floor
Boston, Massachusetts 2116
617-619-5400
tpalmer@charlesbank.com

Managing Director Mark Rosen
Charlesbank Capital Partners, LLC
200 Clarendon Street
54th Floor
Boston, Massachusetts 2116
617-619-5400
mrosen@charlesbank.com

Managing Director Andrew Janower
Charlesbank Capital Partners, LLC
200 Clarendon Street
54th Floor
Boston, Massachusetts 2116
617-619-5400
ajanower@charlesbank.com

Managing Director Kim Davis
Charlesbank Capital Partners, LLC
70 E. 55th Street
20th Floor
New York, New York 10022
212-903-1880
kdavis@charlesbank.com

Managing Director Jon Biotti
Charlesbank Capital Partners, LLC
200 Clarendon Street
54th Floor
Boston, Massachusetts 2116
617-619-5400
jbiotti@charlesbank.com

Managing Director Michael Choe
Charlesbank Capital Partners, LLC
200 Clarendon Street
54th Floor
Boston, Massachusetts 2116
617-619-5400
mchoe@charlesbank.com

VENTURE CAPITAL DIRECTORY

Managing Director Brandon White
Charlesbank Capital Partners, LLC
200 Clarendon Street
54th Floor
Boston, Massachusetts 2116
617-619-5400
bwhite@charlesbank.com

Vice President Samuel Bartlett
Charlesbank Capital Partners, LLC
200 Clarendon Street
54th Floor
Boston, Massachusetts 2116
617-619-5400
sbartlett@charlesbank.com

Vice President Joshua Klevens
Charlesbank Capital Partners, LLC
200 Clarendon Street
54th Floor
Boston, Massachusetts 2116
617-619-5400
jklevens@charlesbank.com

Vice President J. Ryan Carroll
Charlesbank Capital Partners, LLC
200 Clarendon Street
54th Floor
Boston, Massachusetts 2116
617-619-5400
rcarroll@charlesbank.com

Chairman Merril Halpern
Charterhouse Group, Inc.
535 Madison Avenue
28th Floor
New York, New York 10022-4299
212-584-3200
mhalpern@charterhousegroup.com

Managing Partner Thomas Dircks
Charterhouse Group, Inc.
535 Madison Avenue
28th Floor
New York, New York 10022-4299

VENTURE CAPITAL DIRECTORY

212-584-3200
tdircks@charterhousegroup.com

Strategic Partner Paul Mullan
Charterhouse Group, Inc.
535 Madison Avenue
28th Floor
New York, New York 10022-4299
212-584-3200
pmullan@charterhousegroup.com

Senior Partner William Landuyt
Charterhouse Group, Inc.
535 Madison Avenue
28th Floor
New York, New York 10022-4299
212-584-3200
wlanduyt@charterhousegroup.com

Partner Jay Gates
Charterhouse Group, Inc.
535 Madison Avenue
28th Floor
New York, New York 10022-4299
212-584-3200
jgates@charterhousegroup.com

Partner David Hoffman
Charterhouse Group, Inc.
535 Madison Avenue
28th Floor
New York, New York 10022-4299
212-584-3200
dhoffman@charterhousegroup.com

CFO Cheri Lieberman
Charterhouse Group, Inc.
535 Madison Avenue
28th Floor
New York, New York 10022-4299
212-584-3200
clieberman@charterhousegroup.com

Partner C. Taylor Cole Jr.
Charterhouse Group, Inc.
535 Madison Avenue

VENTURE CAPITAL DIRECTORY

28th Floor
New York, New York 10022-4299
212-584-3200
tcole@charterhousegroup.com

Partner Lori Livers-Hess
Charterhouse Group, Inc.
535 Madison Avenue
28th Floor
New York, New York 10022-4299
212-584-3200
lhess@charterhousegroup.com

Partner Joseph Rhodes
Charterhouse Group, Inc.
535 Madison Avenue
28th Floor
New York, New York 10022-4299
212-584-3200
jrhodes@charterhousegroup.com

Vice President Christian Hensley
Charterhouse Group, Inc.
535 Madison Avenue
28th Floor
New York, New York 10022-4299
212-584-3200
chensley@charterhousegroup.com

Vice President Jennifer Guzman
Charterhouse Group, Inc.
535 Madison Avenue
28th Floor
New York, New York 10022-4299
212-584-3200
jguzman@charterhousegroup.com

Vice President Jake Blumenthal
Charterhouse Group, Inc.
535 Madison Avenue
28th Floor
New York, New York 10022-4299
212-584-3200
jblumenthal@charterhousegroup.com

VENTURE CAPITAL DIRECTORY

Associate Alonzo Sherman
Charterhouse Group, Inc.
535 Madison Avenue
28th Floor
New York, New York 10022-4299
212-584-3200
asherman@charterhousegroup.com

Associate Nishant Bubna
Charterhouse Group, Inc.
535 Madison Avenue
28th Floor
New York, New York 10022-4299
212-584-3200
nbubna@charterhousegroup.com

China
 200050
ShanghaiRoom 104, Building 18
No. 800 Huashan Road
China Seed Ventures
 UngermannRalph
86-21-6225-8579
ralph@cseed.cn

China
 200050
ShanghaiRoom 104, Building 18
No. 800 Huashan Road
China Seed Ventures
 YenEarl
86-21-6225-8579
earl@cseed.cn

China
 200050
ShanghaiRoom 104, Building 18
No. 800 Huashan Road
China Seed Ventures
 KayamaYukihiro
86-21-6225-8579

China
 200050
ShanghaiRoom 104, Building 18

VENTURE CAPITAL DIRECTORY

No. 800 Huashan Road
China Seed Ventures
 LiaoMichael
86-21-6225-8579

China
 200050
ShanghaiRoom 104, Building 18
No. 800 Huashan Road
China Seed Ventures
 TongLucene
86-21-6225-8579

China
 100004
BeijingSuite 516, West Tower China World Trade Center
No. 1 Jianguomenwai Ave.
ChinaEquity Group Inc.
 WangChaoyong
86-10-6505-6280
cywang@chinaequity.net

China
 100004
BeijingSuite 516, West Tower China World Trade Center
No. 1 Jianguomenwai Ave.
ChinaEquity Group Inc.
 HuangWayne
86-10-6505-6280

China
 100004
BeijingSuite 516, West Tower China World Trade Center
No. 1 Jianguomenwai Ave.
ChinaEquity Group Inc.
 WeiWilla
86-10-6505-6280

China
 100004
BeijingSuite 516, West Tower China World Trade Center
No. 1 Jianguomenwai Ave.
ChinaEquity Group Inc.
 HuangChristine

VENTURE CAPITAL DIRECTORY

86-10-6505-6280

Chairman and Senior Managing Director David Jones Jr.
Chrysalis Ventures
101 South Fifth Street
Suite 1650
Louisville, Kentucky 40202
502-583-7644
djones@chrysalisventures.com

Managing Director Robert Saunders
Chrysalis Ventures
101 South Fifth Street
Suite 1650
Louisville, Kentucky 40202
502-583-7644
bsaunders@chrysalisventures.com

Senior Advisor Irving Bailey
Chrysalis Ventures
101 South Fifth Street
Suite 1650
Louisville, Kentucky 40202
502-583-7644
ibailey@chrysalisventures.com

Managing Director Koleman Karleski
Chrysalis Ventures
101 South Fifth Street
Suite 1650
Louisville, Kentucky 40202
502-583-7644
koleman@chrysalisventures.com

Principal Wright Steenrod
Chrysalis Ventures
101 South Fifth Street
Suite 1650
Louisville, Kentucky 40202
502-583-7644
wsteenrod@chrysalisventures.com

Analyst Todd Higgerson
Chrysalis Ventures
101 South Fifth Street
Suite 1650

VENTURE CAPITAL DIRECTORY

Louisville, Kentucky 40202
502-583-7644
thiggerson@chrysalisventures.com

Associate Matthew Winn
Chrysalis Ventures
101 South Fifth Street
Suite 1650
Louisville, Kentucky 40202
502-583-7644
mwinn@chrysalisventures.com

Vice President of Finance and Administration Lisa Aly
Chrysalis Ventures
101 South Fifth Street
Suite 1650
Louisville, Kentucky 40202
502-583-7644
laly@chrysalisventures.com

Associate David Parento
Chrysalis Ventures
101 South Fifth Street
Suite 1650
Louisville, Kentucky 40202
502-583-7644
dparento@chrysalisventures.com

General Partner Marshall Payne
CIC Partners, LP
500 Crescent Court
Suite 250
Dallas, Texas 75201
214-871-6807
mpayne@cicpartners.com

Managing Partner Michael Rawlings
CIC Partners, LP
500 Crescent Court
Suite 250
Dallas, Texas 75201
214-871-6807
mrawlings@cicpartners.com

VENTURE CAPITAL DIRECTORY

General Partner Drew Johnson
CIC Partners, LP
500 Crescent Court
Suite 250
Dallas, Texas 75201
214-871-6807
djohnson@cicpartners.com

General Partner Fouad Bashour
CIC Partners, LP
500 Crescent Court
Suite 250
Dallas, Texas 75201
214-871-6807
fbashour@cicpartners.com

Partner Aaron Enrico
CIC Partners, LP
500 Crescent Court
Suite 250
Dallas, Texas 75201
214-871-6807
aenrico@cicpartners.com

Associate Jonathan Dyer
CIC Partners, LP
500 Crescent Court
Suite 250
Dallas, Texas 75201
214-871-6807
jdyer@cicpartners.com

Associate Clayton Spencer
CIC Partners, LP
500 Crescent Court
Suite 250
Dallas, Texas 75201
214-871-6807
cspencer@cicpartners.com

CIM Creative Industries Management Ltd.
Managing Director Heikki Masalin
Unioninkatu 22, 2nd Floor
FI-00130 Helsinki
Finland
358-9-673-889

VENTURE CAPITAL DIRECTORY

heikki.masalin@cimfunds.com

CIM Creative Industries Management Ltd.
Executive Chairman Jorma Routti
Unioninkatu 22, 2nd Floor
FI-00130 Helsinki
Finland
358-9-673-889
jorma.routti@cimfunds.com

Partner Hugh Langmuir
Cinven Ltd.
4, square Edouard VII
FR-75009 Paris
France
33-1-4471-4444

Partner Nicolas Paulmier
Cinven Ltd.
4, square Edouard VII
FR-75009 Paris
France
33-1-4471-4444

Cinven Ltd.
Partner Peter Gangsted
Main Tower
Neue Mainzer Strasse 52
DE-60311 Frankfurt am Main
Germany
49-69-90027-0

Partner Roberto Italia
Cinven Ltd.
Via Manzoni, 30
IT-20121 Milan
Italy
39-2-3211-1700

Managing Partner Robin Hall
Cinven Ltd.
Warwick Court
Paternoster Square
London
EC4M 7AG
United Kingdom

VENTURE CAPITAL DIRECTORY

44-20-7661-3333
robin.hall@cinven.com

Partner Jonathan Clarke
Cinven Ltd.
Warwick Court
Paternoster Square
London
EC4M 7AG
United Kingdom
44-20-7661-3333
jonathan.clarke@cinven.com

Partner Guy Davison
Cinven Ltd.
Warwick Court
Paternoster Square
London
EC4M 7AG
United Kingdom
44-20-7661-3333
guy.davison@cinven.com

Partner Andrew Joy
Cinven Ltd.
Warwick Court
Paternoster Square
London
EC4M 7AG
United Kingdom
44-20-7661-3333
andrew.joy@cinven.com

Partner Simon Rowlands
Cinven Ltd.
Warwick Court
Paternoster Square
London
EC4M 7AG
United Kingdom
44-20-7661-3333
simon.rowlands@cinven.com

Partner Yagnish Chotai
Cinven Ltd.
Warwick Court

VENTURE CAPITAL DIRECTORY

Paternoster Square
London
EC4M 7AG
United Kingdom
44-20-7661-3333
yagnish.chotai@cinven.com

Partner Brian Linden
Cinven Ltd.
Warwick Court
Paternoster Square
London
EC4M 7AG
United Kingdom
44-20-7661-3333

Partner Christian Dosch
Cinven Ltd.
Warwick Court
Paternoster Square
London
EC4M 7AG
United Kingdom
44-20-7661-3333

Managing Director and Group Head, Corporate Finance Richard Kinlough
CIT Corporate Finance, Canada
207 Queen's Quay West
Suite 700
Toronto Ontario M5J 1A7
Canada
416-507-5104
richard.kinlough@cit.com

Partner Daniel Helle
CIVC Partners, LLC
191 North Wacker Drive
Suite 1100
Chicago, Illinois 60606
312-873-7300
dhelle@civc.com

VENTURE CAPITAL DIRECTORY

Partner Christopher Perry
CIVC Partners, LLC
191 North Wacker Drive
Suite 1100
Chicago, Illinois 60606
312-873-7300
cperry@civc.com

Partner Marcus Wedner
CIVC Partners, LLC
191 North Wacker Drive
Suite 1100
Chicago, Illinois 60606
312-873-7300
marcus.wedner@civc.com

Partner Keith Yamada
CIVC Partners, LLC
191 North Wacker Drive
Suite 1100
Chicago, Illinois 60606
312-873-7300
kyamada@civc.com

Principal John Compall
CIVC Partners, LLC
191 North Wacker Drive
Suite 1100
Chicago, Illinois 60606
312-873-7300
jcompall@civc.com

Partner Michael Miller
CIVC Partners, LLC
191 North Wacker Drive
Suite 1100
Chicago, Illinois 60606
312-873-7300
mmiller@civc.com

Principal David Miller
CIVC Partners, LLC
191 North Wacker Drive
Suite 1100
Chicago, Illinois 60606
312-873-7300

VENTURE CAPITAL DIRECTORY

dmiller@civc.com

Vice President Chris McLaughlin
CIVC Partners, LLC
191 North Wacker Drive
Suite 1100
Chicago, Illinois 60606
312-873-7300
cmclaughlin@civc.com

Korea
138-858Seoul 15th Floor, Woonam Building 1329-4, Yeoksam-Dong, Seocho-Gu
CJ Venture Investment
Shin K.Y.President
82-2-3441-5100
kyshin@cj.net

Korea
135-080Seoul 154-11, Samsung-dong Kangnam-Gu
CKD Venture Capital Corporation
Lee Yoon-SikPresident
82-2-3453-3331

CFO Tom Niehaus
Clarion Capital Corporation
Ohio Savings Plaza
1801 East 9th Street, Suite 1120
Cleveland, Ohio 44114
216-687-1096
tom@clariongrp.com

Managing Partner Marc Utay
Clarion Capital Partners, LLC
110 E. 59th St.
Suite 2100
New York, New York 10022
212-821-0111
mutay@clarion-capital.com

Partner Eric Kogan
Clarion Capital Partners, LLC
110 E. 59th St.
Suite 2100
New York, New York 10022
212-821-0111

VENTURE CAPITAL DIRECTORY

ekogan@clarion-capital.com

Principal Jonathan Haas
Clarion Capital Partners, LLC
110 E. 59th St.
Suite 2100
New York, New York 10022
212-821-0111
jhaas@clarion-capital.com

Principal David Ragins
Clarion Capital Partners, LLC
110 E. 59th St.
Suite 2100
New York, New York 10022
212-821-0111
dragins@clarion-capital.com

Principal Thomas Goundrey Jr.
Clarion Capital Partners, LLC
110 E. 59th St.
Suite 2100
New York, New York 10022
212-821-0111
tgoundrey@clarion-capital.com

Matthew Feldman
Clarion Capital Partners, LLC
110 E. 59th St.
Suite 2100
New York, New York 10022
212-821-0111
mfeldman@clarion-capital.com

Adam Schlesinger
Clarion Capital Partners, LLC
110 E. 59th St.
Suite 2100
New York, New York 10022
212-821-0111
aschlesinger@clarion-capital.com

Edward Martin
Clarion Capital Partners, LLC
110 E. 59th St.
Suite 2100

VENTURE CAPITAL DIRECTORY

New York, New York 10022
212-821-0111
emartin@clarion-capital.com

Managing General Partner David Lee
Clarity Partners, L.P.
100 North Crescent Drive
Beverly Hills, California 90210
310-432-0100
dlee@claritypartners.net

Managing General Partner Barry Porter
Clarity Partners, L.P.
100 North Crescent Drive
Beverly Hills, California 90210
310-432-0100
bp@claritypartners.net

Managing General Partner Stephen Rader
Clarity Partners, L.P.
100 North Crescent Drive
Beverly Hills, California 90210
310-432-0100
spr@claritypartners.net

Managing General Partner R. Rudolph Reinfrank
Clarity Partners, L.P.
100 North Crescent Drive
Beverly Hills, California 90210
310-432-0100
rrr@claritypartners.net

General Partner Joshua Gutfreund
Clarity Partners, L.P.
100 North Crescent Drive
Beverly Hills, California 90210
310-432-0100
jlg@claritypartners.net

General Partner Clinton Walker
Clarity Partners, L.P.
100 North Crescent Drive
Beverly Hills, California 90210
310-432-0100
cww@claritypartners.net

VENTURE CAPITAL DIRECTORY

Associate Karan Suri
Clarity Partners, L.P.
100 North Crescent Drive
Beverly Hills, California 90210
310-432-0100
ks@claritypartners.net

Associate Vikram Maniar
Clarity Partners, L.P.
100 North Crescent Drive
Beverly Hills, California 90210
310-432-0100
vcm@claritypartners.net

Senior Vice President Erez Barnavon
Clarity Partners, L.P.
100 North Crescent Drive
Beverly Hills, California 90210
310-432-0100
eb@claritypartners.net

Vice President Leo Griffin
Clarity Partners, L.P.
100 North Crescent Drive
Beverly Hills, California 90210
310-432-0100
lg@claritypartners.net

Managing Partner John Snook
Close Brothers Private Equity LLP
10 Throgmorton Avenue
London
EC2N 2DL
United Kingdom
44-20-7065-1100
john.snook@cbpel.com

Partner Neil Murphy
Close Brothers Private Equity LLP
10 Throgmorton Avenue
London
EC2N 2DL
United Kingdom
44-20-7065-1100
neil.murphy@cbpel.com

VENTURE CAPITAL DIRECTORY

Partner Nick MacNay
Close Brothers Private Equity LLP
10 Throgmorton Avenue
London
EC2N 2DL
United Kingdom
44-20-7065-1100
nick.macnay@cbpel.com

Partner Simon Wildig
Close Brothers Private Equity LLP
10 Throgmorton Avenue
London
EC2N 2DL
United Kingdom
44-20-7065-1100
simon.wildig@cbpel.com

Partner Iain Slater
Close Brothers Private Equity LLP
10 Throgmorton Avenue
London
EC2N 2DL
United Kingdom
44-20-7065-1100
iain.slater@cbpel.com

Investment Director Mark Perryman
Close Brothers Private Equity LLP
10 Throgmorton Avenue
London
EC2N 2DL
United Kingdom
44-20-7065-1100
mark.perryman@cbpel.com

Partner Sean Dinnen
Close Brothers Private Equity LLP
10 Throgmorton Avenue
London
EC2N 2DL
United Kingdom
44-20-7065-1100
sean.dinnen@cbpel.com

Investment Director John Fisher

VENTURE CAPITAL DIRECTORY

Close Brothers Private Equity LLP
10 Throgmorton Avenue
London
EC2N 2DL
United Kingdom
44-20-7065-1100
john.fisher@cbpel.com

Investment Director Mathew Hutchinson
Close Brothers Private Equity LLP
10 Throgmorton Avenue
London
EC2N 2DL
United Kingdom
44-20-7065-1100
mathew.hutchinson@cbpel.com

Investment Manager Ben Alexander
Close Brothers Private Equity LLP
10 Throgmorton Avenue
London
EC2N 2DL
United Kingdom
44-20-7065-1100
ben.alexander@cbpel.com

Investment Manager Andrew Nelson
Close Brothers Private Equity LLP
10 Throgmorton Avenue
London
EC2N 2DL
United Kingdom
44-20-7065-1100
andrew.nelson@cbpel.com

Managing Partner Samuel Schwartz
Comcast Interactive Capital Group
1500 Market Street 42W
Philadelphia, Pennsylvania 19102-2196
215-981-8450
sschwartz@comcast.com

Managing Director Louis Toth
Comcast Interactive Capital Group
1500 Market Street 42W
Philadelphia, Pennsylvania 19102-2196

VENTURE CAPITAL DIRECTORY

215-981-8450
ltoth@comcast.com

CFO Adam Black
Comcast Interactive Capital Group
1500 Market Street 42W
Philadelphia, Pennsylvania 19102-2196
215-981-8450
ablack@comcast.com

Principal David Horowitz
Comcast Interactive Capital Group
1500 Market Street 42W
Philadelphia, Pennsylvania 19102-2196
215-981-8450
dhorowitz@comcast.com

Principal Deepak Sindwani
Comcast Interactive Capital Group
1500 Market Street 42W
Philadelphia, Pennsylvania 19102-2196
215-981-8450

Entrepreneur in Residence Josh Kopelman
Comcast Interactive Capital Group
1500 Market Street 42W
Philadelphia, Pennsylvania 19102-2196
215-981-8450

Founding Partner Julian Brodsky
Comcast Interactive Capital Group
1500 Market Street 42W
Philadelphia, Pennsylvania 19102-2196
215-981-8450
jab@comcast.com

Strategic Advisor Mark Coblitz
Comcast Interactive Capital Group
1500 Market Street 42W
Philadelphia, Pennsylvania 19102-2196
215-981-8450
mcoblitz@comcast.com

Senior Associate David Zilberman
Comcast Interactive Capital Group
1500 Market Street 42W

VENTURE CAPITAL DIRECTORY

Philadelphia, Pennsylvania 19102-2196
215-981-8450

CEO Raja Shamsul Kamal
Commerce Asset Ventures Sdn. Bhd.
6 Commerce House
22-24 Jalan Sri Semantan Satu, Damansara Heights
Kuala Lumpur 50490
Malaysia
60-3-2732-5577

COO Yu Lian Lee
Commerce Asset Ventures Sdn. Bhd.
6 Commerce House
22-24 Jalan Sri Semantan Satu, Damansara Heights
Kuala Lumpur 50490
Malaysia
60-3-2732-5577

Fund Manager Jason See Chin Lam
Commerce Asset Ventures Sdn. Bhd.
6 Commerce House
22-24 Jalan Sri Semantan Satu, Damansara Heights
Kuala Lumpur 50490
Malaysia
60-3-2732-5577
jason@commerce-ventures.com.my

Fund Manager Mohd. Jafni
Commerce Asset Ventures Sdn. Bhd.
6 Commerce House
22-24 Jalan Sri Semantan Satu, Damansara Heights
Kuala Lumpur 50490
Malaysia
60-3-2732-5577

Chairman and CEO J. Patrick Michaels
Communications Equity Associates
101 East Kennedy Boulevard
Suite 3300
Tampa, Florida 33602
813-226-8844
rmichaels@ceaworldwide.com

Vice Chairman Harold Ewen
Communications Equity Associates

VENTURE CAPITAL DIRECTORY

101 East Kennedy Boulevard
Suite 3300
Tampa, Florida 33602
813-226-8844
hewen@ceaworldwide.com

CFO Ming Jung
Communications Equity Associates
101 East Kennedy Boulevard
Suite 3300
Tampa, Florida 33602
813-226-8844
mjung@ceaworldwide.com

Controller Angela Horwitz
Communications Equity Associates
101 East Kennedy Boulevard
Suite 3300
Tampa, Florida 33602
813-226-8844
ahorwitz@ceaworldwide.com

Managing Director Jose Rodriguez
Communications Equity Associates
150 S.E. 2nd Ave
Suite 609
Miami, Florida 33131
305-810-2740
jrodriguez@ceaworldwide.com

President and Managing Director Michael Miller
ComSpace Development, LLC
12521 Manderley Way
Oak Hill, Virginia 20171
703-716-0675
mmiller@comspacedev.com

Director W. Theodore Pierson Jr.
ComSpace Development, LLC
12521 Manderley Way
Oak Hill, Virginia 20171
703-716-0675

VENTURE CAPITAL DIRECTORY

Senior Managing Director Clifford Friedman
Constellation Ventures
383 Madison Avenue
28th Floor
New York, New York 10179
212-272-2728
cfriedman@bear.com

Managing Director Liza Boyd
Constellation Ventures
383 Madison Avenue
28th Floor
New York, New York 10179
212-272-2728
lboyd@bear.com

Managing Director Tom Wasserman
Constellation Ventures
383 Madison Avenue
28th Floor
New York, New York 10179
212-272-2728
twasserman@bear.com

Vice President Bryan Rubin
Constellation Ventures
383 Madison Avenue
28th Floor
New York, New York 10179
212-272-2728
brubin@bear.com

Content Capital Ltd.
Tim Benjamin
Level 3, 4-14 Foster Street
Surry Hills New South Wales 2010
Australia
61-2-9281-8665

Content Capital Ltd.
David Court
Level 3, 4-14 Foster Street
Surry Hills New South Wales 2010
Australia
61-2-9281-8665

VENTURE CAPITAL DIRECTORY

Senior Managing Director Yuval Almog
Coral Capital Management
60 South Sixth Street
Suite 3510
Minneapolis, Minnesota 55402
612-335-8698
yuval@coralcm.com

Managing Director Todd Ortberg
Coral Capital Management
60 South Sixth Street
Suite 3510
Minneapolis, Minnesota 55402
612-335-8698
todd@coralcm.com

Managing Director/CFO Linda Watchmaker
Coral Capital Management
60 South Sixth Street
Suite 3510
Minneapolis, Minnesota 55402
612-335-8698
linda@coralcm.com

Managing Director/General Counsel Mark Headrick
Coral Capital Management
60 South Sixth Street
Suite 3510
Minneapolis, Minnesota 55402
612-335-8698
mark@coralcm.com

Managing Director Steve Gordon
Coral Capital Management
60 South Sixth Street
Suite 3510
Minneapolis, Minnesota 55402
612-335-8698
steve@coralcm.com

Venture Partner Robert Majteles
Coral Capital Management
60 South Sixth Street
Suite 3510
Minneapolis, Minnesota 55402
612-335-8698

VENTURE CAPITAL DIRECTORY

rob@coralcm.com

Senior Research Associate Christopher Smith
Coral Capital Management
60 South Sixth Street
Suite 3510
Minneapolis, Minnesota 55402
612-335-8698
chris@coralcm.com

Entrepreneur-in-Residence Ben Joseph
Coral Capital Management
60 South Sixth Street
Suite 3510
Minneapolis, Minnesota 55402
612-335-8698
ben@coralcm.com

Senior Research Associate Ori Levy
Coral Capital Management
60 South Sixth Street
Suite 3510
Minneapolis, Minnesota 55402
612-335-8698
ori@coralcm.com

Managing General Partner James Murray Jr.
Court Square Ventures, LLC
Zero Court Square
Charlottesville, Virginia 22902
804-817-3300
jmurray@courtsquareventures.com

General Partner Randy Castleman
Court Square Ventures, LLC
Zero Court Square
Charlottesville, Virginia 22902
804-817-3300
rcastleman@courtsquareventures.com

General Partner Chris Holden
Court Square Ventures, LLC
Zero Court Square
Charlottesville, Virginia 22902
804-817-3300

VENTURE CAPITAL DIRECTORY

cholden@courtsquareventures.com

Principal and CFO Douglas Burns
Court Square Ventures, LLC
Zero Court Square
Charlottesville, Virginia 22902
804-817-3300
dburns@courtsquareventures.com

Associate Brian Kannry
Court Square Ventures, LLC
Zero Court Square
Charlottesville, Virginia 22902
804-817-3300
bkannry@courtsquareventures.com

Investment Manager Henry Fyson
Creative Capital Fund
Dilke House
1 Malet St
London
WC1E 7JN
United Kingdom
44-870-909-6333
henry@ccfund.co.uk

Investment Manager Joanne Evans
Creative Capital Fund
Dilke House
1 Malet St
London
WC1E 7JN
United Kingdom
44-870-909-6333
joanne@ccfund.co.uk

Chairman Fred Mendelsohn
Creative Capital Fund
Dilke House
1 Malet St
London
WC1E 7JN
United Kingdom
44-870-909-6333
fred@ccfund.co.uk

VENTURE CAPITAL DIRECTORY

Investment Adviser John Sanderson
Creative Capital Fund
Dilke House
1 Malet St
London
WC1E 7JN
United Kingdom
44-870-909-6333

Investment Adviser Rose Lewis
Creative Capital Fund
Dilke House
1 Malet St
London
WC1E 7JN
United Kingdom
44-870-909-6333

Managing Partner Peter Chan
Crest Capital Partners
50 Raffles Place #34-03
Singapore Land Tower
 48623
Singapore
65-6533-2002
peter.chan@crest-capital.com

Investment Partner Thian Sze Yong
Crest Capital Partners
50 Raffles Place #34-03
Singapore Land Tower
 48623
Singapore
65-6533-2002
ts.yong@crest-capital.com

Investment Partner Caroline Wee
Crest Capital Partners
50 Raffles Place #34-03
Singapore Land Tower
 48623
Singapore
65-6533-2002
caroline.wee@crest-capital.com

Japan

VENTURE CAPITAL DIRECTORY

107-0062
TokyoRiviera Minami Aoyama Building 5th Floor
3-3-3 Minami-Aoyama Minato-ku
CSK Venture Capital Co. Ltd.
IshimuraShunichi
81-3-5771-6411
ishimura@cskvc.co.jp

Japan
107-0062
TokyoRiviera Minami Aoyama Building 5th Floor
3-3-3 Minami-Aoyama Minato-ku
CSK Venture Capital Co. Ltd.
KaneshiroMakoto
81-3-5771-6411
kaneshiro@cskvc.co.jp

President and CEO William Custer
Custer Capital, Inc.
14 South High Street
P.O. Box 673
New Albany, Ohio 43054
614-855-9980
wcuster@custercapital.com

Director - Operations and Compliance Martha Kashner
Custer Capital, Inc.
14 South High Street
P.O. Box 673
New Albany, Ohio 43054
614-855-9980
mkashner@custercapital.com

Managing Director Donald O'Shea
Custer Capital, Inc.
14 South High Street
P.O. Box 673
New Albany, Ohio 43054
614-855-9980
doshea@custercapital.com

Chairman and CEO James Stern
Cypress Group LLC
65 East 55th Street
28th Floor
New York, New York 10022

VENTURE CAPITAL DIRECTORY

212-705-0150
jstern@cypressgp.com

Vice Chairman Jeffrey Hughes
Cypress Group LLC
65 East 55th Street
28th Floor
New York, New York 10022
212-705-0150
jhughes@cypressgp.com

Managing Director Michael Finley
Cypress Group LLC
65 East 55th Street
28th Floor
New York, New York 10022
212-705-0150
mfinley@cypressgp.com

Managing Director Christopher Harned
Cypress Group LLC
65 East 55th Street
28th Floor
New York, New York 10022
212-705-0150
charned@cypressgp.com

Managing Director Joseph Parzick
Cypress Group LLC
65 East 55th Street
28th Floor
New York, New York 10022
212-705-0150
jparzick@cypressgp.com

Principal Walter Keenan
Cypress Group LLC
65 East 55th Street
28th Floor
New York, New York 10022
212-705-0150
wkeenan@cypressgp.com

Associate Aditya Talwar
Cypress Group LLC
65 East 55th Street

VENTURE CAPITAL DIRECTORY

28th Floor
New York, New York 10022
212-705-0150
atalwar@cypressgp.com

Vice President Jonathan Saltzman
Cypress Group LLC
65 East 55th Street
28th Floor
New York, New York 10022
212-705-0150
jsaltzman@cypressgp.com

CEO Richard Frank
Darby Overseas Investments, Ltd.
1133 Connecticut Avenue, N.W.
Suite 400
Washington, District of Columbia 20036
202-872-0500

Senior Managing Director - Americas Julio Lastres
Darby Overseas Investments, Ltd.
1133 Connecticut Avenue, N.W.
Suite 400
Washington, District of Columbia 20036
202-872-0500

Managing Director Jaime Salinas Solano
Darby Overseas Investments, Ltd.
1133 Connecticut Avenue, N.W.
Suite 400
Washington, District of Columbia 20036
202-872-0500

Principal Jonathan Whittle
Darby Overseas Investments, Ltd.
1133 Connecticut Avenue, N.W.
Suite 400
Washington, District of Columbia 20036
202-872-0500
jwhittle@doil.com

Managing Partner Curtis Rocca III
DCA Capital Partners, LP
3721 Douglas Boulevard
Suite 350

VENTURE CAPITAL DIRECTORY

Roseville, California 95661
916-960-5350
crocca@dcapartners.com

Partner Jeremy Wolfe
DCA Capital Partners, LP
3721 Douglas Boulevard
Suite 350
Roseville, California 95661
916-960-5350
jwolfe@dcacapital.com

General Partner Steven Mills
DCA Capital Partners, LP
3721 Douglas Boulevard
Suite 350
Roseville, California 95661
916-960-5350
smills@dcacapital.com

China
 100738
BeijingUnit 1, Level 10, Tower W2, Oriental Plaza
No.1 East Chang An Ave., Dong Cheng District
DCM
 LinHurst
86-10-8515-1180
hurst@dcm.com

Co-Founder and General Partner Dixon Doll
DCM
2420 Sand Hill Road
Suite 200
Menlo Park, California 94025
650-233-1400
dixon@dcm.com

Co-Founder and General Partner David Chao
DCM
2420 Sand Hill Road
Suite 200
Menlo Park, California 94025
650-233-1400
dchao@dcm.com

General Partner Peter Moran

VENTURE CAPITAL DIRECTORY

DCM
2420 Sand Hill Road
Suite 200
Menlo Park, California 94025
650-233-1400
pmoran@dcm.com

General Partner Rob Theis
DCM
2420 Sand Hill Road
Suite 200
Menlo Park, California 94025
650-233-1400
rtheis@dcm.com

General Partner Tom Blaisdell
DCM
2420 Sand Hill Road
Suite 200
Menlo Park, California 94025
650-233-1400
tblaisdell@dcm.com

General Partner Carl Amdahl
DCM
2420 Sand Hill Road
Suite 200
Menlo Park, California 94025
650-233-1400
carl@dcm.com

Partner Ruby Lu
DCM
2420 Sand Hill Road
Suite 200
Menlo Park, California 94025
650-233-1400
ruby@dcm.com

Principal Gen Isayama
DCM
2420 Sand Hill Road
Suite 200
Menlo Park, California 94025
650-233-1400
gen@dcm.com

VENTURE CAPITAL DIRECTORY

Venture Partner Bob Hawk
DCM
2420 Sand Hill Road
Suite 200
Menlo Park, California 94025
650-233-1400
bhawk@dcm.com

Associate Michael Blaustein
DCM
2420 Sand Hill Road
Suite 200
Menlo Park, California 94025
650-233-1400
mblaustein@dcm.com

Associate Michelle Wu
DCM
2420 Sand Hill Road
Suite 200
Menlo Park, California 94025
650-233-1400
mwu@dcm.com

Managing Director Ross George
Direct Capital Private Equity Ltd.
PO Box 6466, Wellesley Street
Auckland
New Zealand
64-9-307-2562
ross.george@directcapital.co.nz

Director Mark Hutton
Direct Capital Private Equity Ltd.
PO Box 6466, Wellesley Street
Auckland
New Zealand
64-9-307-2562
mark.hutton@directcapital.co.nz

Director Bill Kermode
Direct Capital Private Equity Ltd.
PO Box 6466, Wellesley Street
Auckland
New Zealand
64-9-307-2562

VENTURE CAPITAL DIRECTORY

bill.kermode@directcapital.co.nz

Investment Director - TMT Ventures Gavin Lonergan
Direct Capital Private Equity Ltd.
PO Box 6466, Wellesley Street
Auckland
New Zealand
64-9-307-2562
gavin.lonergan@directcapital.co.nz

Investment Director - TMT Ventures Kory Fagan
Direct Capital Private Equity Ltd.
PO Box 6466, Wellesley Street
Auckland
New Zealand
64-9-307-2562
kory.fagan@directcapital.co.nz

Investment Director Tony Batterton
Direct Capital Private Equity Ltd.
PO Box 6466, Wellesley Street
Auckland
New Zealand
64-9-307-2562
tony.batterton@directcapital.co.nz

Chief Executive - TMT Ventures Paul van Tol
Direct Capital Private Equity Ltd.
PO Box 6466, Wellesley Street
Auckland
New Zealand
64-9-307-2562

Finance Manager Esther Bass
Direct Capital Private Equity Ltd.
PO Box 6466, Wellesley Street
Auckland
New Zealand
64-9-307-2562
esther.bass@directcapital.co.nz

Investment Manager Simon Plowman
Direct Capital Private Equity Ltd.
PO Box 6466, Wellesley Street
Auckland
New Zealand

VENTURE CAPITAL DIRECTORY

64-9-307-2562
simon.plowman@directcapital.co.nz

Managing Partner Nenad Marovac
DN Capital
28 St. James' Square
London
SW1Y 4JH
United Kingdom
44-20-7451-2800
nenad@dncapital.com

Managing Partner Steve Schlenker
DN Capital
28 St. James' Square
London
SW1Y 4JH
United Kingdom
44-20-7451-2800
steve@dncapital.com

Investment Manager Cedric Sellin
DN Capital
28 St. James' Square
London
SW1Y 4JH
United Kingdom
44-20-7451-2800
cedric@dncapital.com

Analyst Andy Choi
DN Capital
28 St. James' Square
London
SW1Y 4JH
United Kingdom
44-20-7451-2800
andy@dncapital.com

Arie Rosenfeld
DOR Ventures
16 Hagalim Ave.
Delta House, 2nd Floor
Herzliya 46733
Israel
972-9-957-8595

VENTURE CAPITAL DIRECTORY

Ilan Neugarten
DOR Ventures
16 Hagalim Ave.
Delta House, 2nd Floor
Herzliya 46733
Israel
972-9-957-8595
ineugarten@dorventures.com

Doughty Hanson Technology Ventures
Investment Manager Stefan Tirtey
Schäfflerhof
Windenmacherstrasse 2
DE-80333 Munich
Germany
49-89-2444-06-0
stefan.tirtey@doughtyhanson.com

Managing Director Nigel Grierson
Doughty Hanson Technology Ventures
45 Pall Mall
London
SW1Y 5JG
United Kingdom
44-20-7663-9300
nigel.grierson@doughtyhanson.com

Managing Director George Powlick
Doughty Hanson Technology Ventures
45 Pall Mall
London
SW1Y 5JG
United Kingdom
44-20-7663-9300
george.powlick@doughtyhanson.com

Principal Ivan Farneti
Doughty Hanson Technology Ventures
45 Pall Mall
London
SW1Y 5JG
United Kingdom
44-20-7663-9300
ivan.farneti@doughtyhanson.com

Principal Jerry Ennis

VENTURE CAPITAL DIRECTORY

Doughty Hanson Technology Ventures
45 Pall Mall
London
SW1Y 5JG
United Kingdom
44-20-7663-9300
jerry.ennis@doughtyhanson.com

Principal Soren Hein
Doughty Hanson Technology Ventures
45 Pall Mall
London
SW1Y 5JG
United Kingdom
44-20-7663-9300
soren.hein@doughtyhanson.com

Analyst Sitar Teli
Doughty Hanson Technology Ventures
45 Pall Mall
London
SW1Y 5JG
United Kingdom
44-20-7663-9300
sitar.teli@doughtyhanson.com

Principal Don Millen Jr.
Dragonfly Capital Partners
The Packard Building
1310 S. Tryon Street, Suite 109
Charlotte, North Carolina 28203
704-342-3491
don@dragonflycapital.com

Principal Rene Matthews-Usher
Dragonfly Capital Partners
The Packard Building
1310 S. Tryon Street, Suite 109
Charlotte, North Carolina 28203
704-342-3491
rene@dragonflycapital.com

Randy Snyder
Dragonfly Capital Partners
The Packard Building
1310 S. Tryon Street, Suite 109

VENTURE CAPITAL DIRECTORY

Charlotte, North Carolina 28203
704-342-3491
randy@dragonflycapital.com

Jeffrey Singer
Dragonfly Capital Partners
The Graybar Building
420 Lexington Avenue, Suite 2620
New York, New York 10170
646-383-8605
jeffrey@dragonflycapital.com

China
 200333
ShanghaiUnit 303, Building 27
879 Zhongjiang Road
Dragonvest Partners, LP
 LiCha
86-21-6142-3234
chali@dragonvestpartners.com

China
 200333
ShanghaiUnit 303, Building 27
879 Zhongjiang Road
Dragonvest Partners, LP
 YeAlice
86-21-6142-3234
alice@dragonvestpartners.com

Managing General Partner Jesse Parker
Dragonvest Partners, LP
20 Farnham Circle
Needham, Massachusetts 2492
781-449-9011
jesse@dragonvestpartners.com

Managing Director Ross Goldstein
Draper Fisher Jurvetson Gotham Ventures
132 West 31st Street
Suite 1102
New York, New York 10001
212-279-3980
ross@dfjgotham.com

Managing Director Daniel Schultz

VENTURE CAPITAL DIRECTORY

Draper Fisher Jurvetson Gotham Ventures
132 West 31st Street
Suite 1102
New York, New York 10001
212-279-3980
danny@dfjgotham.com

Managing Director Jed Katz
Draper Fisher Jurvetson Gotham Ventures
132 West 31st Street
Suite 1102
New York, New York 10001
212-279-3980
jed@dfjgotham.com

Associate Thatcher Bell
Draper Fisher Jurvetson Gotham Ventures
132 West 31st Street
Suite 1102
New York, New York 10001
212-279-3980
thatcher@dfjgotham.com

Managing Director Donald Jones
Draper Triangle Ventures, LP
2 Gateway Center
20th Floor
Pittsburgh, Pennsylvania 15222
412-288-9800
djones@dtvc.com

Managing Director Jay Katarincic
Draper Triangle Ventures, LP
2 Gateway Center
20th Floor
Pittsburgh, Pennsylvania 15222
412-288-9800
jay@dtvc.com

Managing Director Michael Stubler
Draper Triangle Ventures, LP
2 Gateway Center
20th Floor
Pittsburgh, Pennsylvania 15222
412-288-9800
mstubler@dtvc.com

VENTURE CAPITAL DIRECTORY

Managing Director D. Thompson Jones
Draper Triangle Ventures, LP
2 Gateway Center
20th Floor
Pittsburgh, Pennsylvania 15222
412-288-9800
tjones@dtvc.com

Managing Director Mark Richey
Draper Triangle Ventures, LP
2 Gateway Center
20th Floor
Pittsburgh, Pennsylvania 15222
412-288-9800
mark@dtvc.com

Director Craig Gomulka
Draper Triangle Ventures, LP
2 Gateway Center
20th Floor
Pittsburgh, Pennsylvania 15222
412-288-9800
craig@dtvc.com

China
 200020
ShanghaiNo.1 Gao Lan Road
DT Capital Partners
 ChenWilliam
86-21-5383-5999
will.chen@dtcap.com

China
 200020
ShanghaiNo.1 Gao Lan Road
DT Capital Partners
 ShawRoman
86-21-5383-5999
roman.shaw@dtcap.com

China
 200020
ShanghaiNo.1 Gao Lan Road
DT Capital Partners
 TianJoe

VENTURE CAPITAL DIRECTORY

86-21-5383-5999
joe.tian@dtcap.com

China
 100005
BeijingRm 1005A, China Resources Building
No 8 Jianguomenbei Avenue
DT Capital Partners
 ZhaoJun
86-10-8519-2121
jun.zhao@dtcap.com

General Partner Greg Penner
DT Capital Partners
Building 2, Suite 150
3000 Sand Hill Road
Menlo Park, California 94025
650-854-8301
greg.penner@dtcap.com

CEO Dali Sardar
DTA Ventures Management Sdn. Bhd.
24A, Jalan Datuk Sulaiman
Taman Tun Dr. Ismail
Kuala Lumpur 60000
Malaysia
60-3-7722-2560
dali@dtacapital.com

COO K.C. Tan
DTA Ventures Management Sdn. Bhd.
24A, Jalan Datuk Sulaiman
Taman Tun Dr. Ismail
Kuala Lumpur 60000
Malaysia
60-3-7722-2560
kctan@dtacapital.com

CTO Naim Yunus
DTA Ventures Management Sdn. Bhd.
24A, Jalan Datuk Sulaiman
Taman Tun Dr. Ismail
Kuala Lumpur 60000
Malaysia
60-3-7722-2560
naim@dtacapital.com

VENTURE CAPITAL DIRECTORY

CFO Nikhil Kothari
DTA Ventures Management Sdn. Bhd.
24A, Jalan Datuk Sulaiman
Taman Tun Dr. Ismail
Kuala Lumpur 60000
Malaysia
60-3-7722-2560
nikhil@dtacapital.com

Investment Manager Wan Fara
DTA Ventures Management Sdn. Bhd.
24A, Jalan Datuk Sulaiman
Taman Tun Dr. Ismail
Kuala Lumpur 60000
Malaysia
60-3-7722-2560
wan@dtacapital.com

Partner John Duff Jr.
Duff Ackerman & Goodrich, LLC (DAG Private Equity)
Two Embarcadero Center
Suite 2300
San Francisco, California 94111
415-788-2755
jduff@dagllc.com

Partner Arnold Ackerman
Duff Ackerman & Goodrich, LLC (DAG Private Equity)
Two Embarcadero Center
Suite 2300
San Francisco, California 94111
415-788-2755
awa@dagllc.com

Partner R. Thomas Goodrich
Duff Ackerman & Goodrich, LLC (DAG Private Equity)
Two Embarcadero Center
Suite 2300
San Francisco, California 94111
415-788-2755
rtg@dagllc.com

Stanton Dodson
Chairman
Duke Equity Partners

VENTURE CAPITAL DIRECTORY

Dubai International Financial Centre
Level 12, The Gate, P.O. Box 121208
Dubai United Arab Emirates
971-4-361-1949
sdodson@dukeequity.com

Gopal Patwardhan
Managing Partner
Duke Equity Partners
Dubai International Financial Centre
Level 12, The Gate, P.O. Box 121208
Dubai United Arab Emirates
971-4-361-1949
gopal@dukeequity.com

Managing Partner Frédéric Chauffier
Duke Street Capital
9, rue du Faubourg Saint-Honoré
FR-75008 Paris
France
33-1-5343-5444

Partner Mark Foulds
Duke Street Capital
9, rue du Faubourg Saint-Honoré
FR-75008 Paris
France
33-1-5343-5444

Partner Didier Bismuth
Duke Street Capital
9, rue du Faubourg Saint-Honoré
FR-75008 Paris
France
33-1-5343-5444

Managing Partner Peter Talyor
Duke Street Capital
Almack House
28 King Street
London
SW1Y 6XA
United Kingdom
44-20-7451-6600

Partner John Harper

VENTURE CAPITAL DIRECTORY

Duke Street Capital
Almack House
28 King Street
London
SW1Y 6XA
United Kingdom
44-20-7451-6600

Partner Iain Kennedy
Duke Street Capital
Almack House
28 King Street
London
SW1Y 6XA
United Kingdom
44-20-7451-6600
kennedy@dukestreetcapital.com

Partner Timothy Lebus
Duke Street Capital
Almack House
28 King Street
London
SW1Y 6XA
United Kingdom
44-20-7451-6600

Chairman Simon Miller
Dunedin Capital Partners Ltd.
10 George Street
Edinburgh
EH2 2DW
United Kingdom
44-131-225-6699
simon.miller@dunedin.com

Chief Executive Ross Marshall
Dunedin Capital Partners Ltd.
10 George Street
Edinburgh
EH2 2DW
United Kingdom
44-131-225-6699
ross.marshall@dunedin.com

Managing Director, Portfolio Brian Scouler

VENTURE CAPITAL DIRECTORY

Dunedin Capital Partners Ltd.
10 George Street
Edinburgh
EH2 2DW
United Kingdom
44-131-225-6699
brian.scouler@dunedin.com

Director Dougal Bennett
Dunedin Capital Partners Ltd.
28 Savile Row
London
W1S 2EU
United Kingdom
44-20-7292-2110
dougal.bennett@dunedin.com

Managing Director, New Investment Shaun Middleton
Dunedin Capital Partners Ltd.
10 George Street
Edinburgh
EH2 2DW
United Kingdom
44-131-225-6699
shaun.middleton@dunedin.com

Director Duncan Macrae
Dunedin Capital Partners Ltd.
10 George Street
Edinburgh
EH2 2DW
United Kingdom
44-131-225-6699
duncan.macrae@dunedin.com

Director Mark Ligertwood
Dunedin Capital Partners Ltd.
10 George Street
Edinburgh
EH2 2DW
United Kingdom
44-131-225-6699
mark.ligertwood@dunedin.com

Director Nicol Fraser
Dunedin Capital Partners Ltd.

VENTURE CAPITAL DIRECTORY

10 George Street
Edinburgh
EH2 2DW
United Kingdom
44-131-225-6699
nicol.fraser@dunedin.com

Finance Director Graeme Murray
Dunedin Capital Partners Ltd.
10 George Street
Edinburgh
EH2 2DW
United Kingdom
44-131-225-6699
graeme.murray@dunedin.com

Director John Hudson
Dunedin Capital Partners Ltd.
10 George Street
Edinburgh
EH2 2DW
United Kingdom
44-131-225-6699
nicol.fraser@dunedin.com

Investment Manager Andrew Pickup
Dunedin Capital Partners Ltd.
28 Savile Row
London
W1S 2EU
United Kingdom
44-20-7292-2110
andrew.pickup@dunedin.com

Director Giles Derry
Dunedin Capital Partners Ltd.
28 Savile Row
London
W1S 2EU
United Kingdom
44-20-7292-2110
giles.derry@dunedin.com

Managing Partner John Friedman
Easton Capital Investment Group
767 Third Avenue

VENTURE CAPITAL DIRECTORY

7th Floor
New York, New York 10022
212-702-0950
friedman@eastoncapital.com

Managing Director Francisco Garcia
Easton Capital Investment Group
SBS Tower, Suite 750
2601 South Bayshore Drive
Miami, Florida 33133
305-361-6479
garcia@eastoncapital.com

Venture Partner Mark Chen
Easton Capital Investment Group
767 Third Avenue
7th Floor
New York, New York 10022
212-702-0950
chen@eastoncapital.com

Managing Director Charles Hughes III
Easton Capital Investment Group
767 Third Avenue
7th Floor
New York, New York 10022
212-702-0950
hughes@eastoncapital.com

Managing Director Edward Meyer
Easton Capital Investment Group
SBS Tower, Suite 750
2601 South Bayshore Drive
Miami, Florida 33133
305-361-6479
meyer@eastoncapital.com

Managing Director Richard Schneider
Easton Capital Investment Group
767 Third Avenue
7th Floor
New York, New York 10022
212-702-0950
schneider@eastoncapital.com

Principal Daniel Googel

VENTURE CAPITAL DIRECTORY

Easton Capital Investment Group
767 Third Avenue
7th Floor
New York, New York 10022
212-702-0950
googel@eastoncapital.com

Venture Partner Seth Orlow
Easton Capital Investment Group
767 Third Avenue
7th Floor
New York, New York 10022
212-702-0950
orlow@eastoncapital.com

Senior Associate Jimmy Lee
Easton Capital Investment Group
767 Third Avenue
7th Floor
New York, New York 10022
212-702-0950
lee@eastoncapital.com

Senior Associate Anup Arora
Easton Capital Investment Group
767 Third Avenue
7th Floor
New York, New York 10022
212-702-0950
arora@eastoncapital.com

Managing Director and Co-Founder Fred Anderson
Elevation Partners
2800 Sand Hill Road
Suite 160
Menlo Park, California 94025
650-687-6700
fred@elevation.com

Managing Director and Co-Founder Marc Bodnick
Elevation Partners
2800 Sand Hill Road
Suite 160
Menlo Park, California 94025
650-687-6700
marc@elevation.com

VENTURE CAPITAL DIRECTORY

Managing Director and Co-Founder Roger McNamee
Elevation Partners
2800 Sand Hill Road
Suite 160
Menlo Park, California 94025
650-687-6700
roger@elevation.com

Managing Director and Co-Founder Bret Pearlman
Elevation Partners
2800 Sand Hill Road
Suite 160
Menlo Park, California 94025
650-687-6700
bret@elevation.com

Bono
Elevation Partners
2800 Sand Hill Road
Suite 160
Menlo Park, California 94025
650-687-6700

Managing Director, Investor Relations Kevin Albert
Elevation Partners
2800 Sand Hill Road
Suite 160
Menlo Park, California 94025
650-687-6700
kevin@elevation.com

Principal Sherwin Chen
Elevation Partners
2800 Sand Hill Road
Suite 160
Menlo Park, California 94025
650-687-6700
sherwin@elevation.com

Principal Adam Hopkins
Elevation Partners
2800 Sand Hill Road
Suite 160
Menlo Park, California 94025
650-687-6700

VENTURE CAPITAL DIRECTORY

adam@elevation.com

Associate Connie Chan
Elevation Partners
2800 Sand Hill Road
Suite 160
Menlo Park, California 94025
650-687-6700
connie@elevation.com

Principal Patty Halfen
Elevation Partners
2800 Sand Hill Road
Suite 160
Menlo Park, California 94025
650-687-6700
patty@elevation.com

Associate Rohan Nirody
Elevation Partners
2800 Sand Hill Road
Suite 160
Menlo Park, California 94025
650-687-6700
rohan@elevation.com

Principal Martin Fichtner
Elevation Partners
2800 Sand Hill Road
Suite 160
Menlo Park, California 94025
650-687-6700
martin@elevation.com

Associate Robert Cantwell
Elevation Partners
2800 Sand Hill Road
Suite 160
Menlo Park, California 94025
650-687-6700
robert@elevation.com

Associate Jay Kahn
Elevation Partners
2800 Sand Hill Road
Suite 160

VENTURE CAPITAL DIRECTORY

Menlo Park, California 94025
650-687-6700
jay@elevation.com

Associate Tommy Wu
Elevation Partners
2800 Sand Hill Road
Suite 160
Menlo Park, California 94025
650-687-6700
tommy@elevation.com

Chief Executive Conor O'Connor
Enterprise Equity (Irl) Ltd.
Dublin Road
Dundalk
County Louth
Ireland
353-42-933-3167
conor@enterpriseequity.ie

Investment Executive Rory Hynes
Enterprise Equity (Irl) Ltd.
Dublin Road
Dundalk
County Louth
Ireland
353-42-933-3167
rory@enterpriseequity.ie

Investment Executive Eric Reed
Enterprise Equity (Irl) Ltd.
Dublin Road
Dundalk
County Louth
Ireland
353-42-933-3167
eric@enterpriseequity.ie

Investment Executive Tom Shinkwin
Enterprise Equity (Irl) Ltd.
Dublin Road
Dundalk
County Louth
Ireland
353-42-933-3167

VENTURE CAPITAL DIRECTORY

tom@enterpriseequity.ie

Investment Executive Frank Walsh
Enterprise Equity (Irl) Ltd.
Dublin Road
Dundalk
County Louth
Ireland
353-42-933-3167
frank@enterpriseequity.ie

Chairman Robert Faris
Enterprise Investors
Warsaw Financial Center
53 Emilii Plater Street
PL-00113 Warsaw
Poland
48-22-458-8500
robert.faris@ei.com.pl

President Jacek Siwicki
Enterprise Investors
Warsaw Financial Center
53 Emilii Plater Street
PL-00113 Warsaw
Poland
48-22-458-8500
jacek.siwicki@ei.com.pl

Managing Partner Robert Manz
Enterprise Investors
Warsaw Financial Center
53 Emilii Plater Street
PL-00113 Warsaw
Poland
48-22-458-8500
robert.manz@ei.com.pl

Managing Partner Dariusz Pronczuk
Enterprise Investors
Warsaw Financial Center
53 Emilii Plater Street
PL-00113 Warsaw
Poland
48-22-458-8500
dariusz.pronczuk@ei.com.pl

VENTURE CAPITAL DIRECTORY

Managing Partner Michal Rusiecki
Enterprise Investors
Warsaw Financial Center
53 Emilii Plater Street
PL-00113 Warsaw
Poland
48-22-458-8500
michal.rusiecki@ei.com.pl

Managing Partner Ryszard Wojtkowski
Enterprise Investors
Warsaw Financial Center
53 Emilii Plater Street
PL-00113 Warsaw
Poland
48-22-458-8500
ryszard.wojtkowski@ei.com.pl

Partner Piotr Augustyniak
Enterprise Investors
Warsaw Financial Center
53 Emilii Plater Street
PL-00113 Warsaw
Poland
48-22-458-8500
piotr.augustyniak@ei.com.pl

Senior Managing Director John Garel
Envest Ventures, LLC
2101 Parks Avenue
Suite 401
Virginia Beach, Virginia 23451
757-437-3000

Senior Managing Director David Kaufman
Envest Ventures, LLC
2101 Parks Avenue
Suite 401
Virginia Beach, Virginia 23451
757-437-3000
kaufman@envestventures.com

Managing Director Kevin Wilson
Envest Ventures, LLC
2101 Parks Avenue
Suite 401

VENTURE CAPITAL DIRECTORY

Virginia Beach, Virginia 23451
757-437-3000
wilson@envestventures.com

Vice President of Analysis Amanda Hagy
Envest Ventures, LLC
2101 Parks Avenue
Suite 401
Virginia Beach, Virginia 23451
757-437-3000
hagy@envestventures.com

Managing Partner Nicola Bettio
Eontech Ventures S.A.
5 rue Guillaume Kroll
Luxembourg LU-1025
Luxembourg
352-26-4958-4265
nicola.bettio@eontechventures.com

Managing Partner Sandro Grigolli
Eontech Ventures S.A.
5 rue Guillaume Kroll
Luxembourg LU-1025
Luxembourg
352-26-4958-4265
sandro.grigolli@eontechventures.com

Venture Partner James Carter
Eontech Ventures S.A.
5 rue Guillaume Kroll
Luxembourg LU-1025
Luxembourg
352-26-4958-4265
james.carter@eontechventures.com

Equity Partners Management Pty Ltd.
Richard Gregson
Level 12
60 Margaret Street
Sydney New South Wales 2000
Australia
61-2-8298-5100
rgregson@equitypartners.com.au

Equity Partners Management Pty Ltd.

VENTURE CAPITAL DIRECTORY

Rajeev Dhawan
Level 12
60 Margaret Street
Sydney New South Wales 2000
Australia
61-2-8298-5100
rajeev.dhawan@equitypartners.com.au

Equity Partners Management Pty Ltd.
Quentin Jones
Level 12
60 Margaret Street
Sydney New South Wales 2000
Australia
61-2-8298-5100
qbjones@equitypartners.com.au

Equity Partners Management Pty Ltd.
Kim Durack
Level 12
60 Margaret Street
Sydney New South Wales 2000
Australia
61-2-8298-5100
kim.durack@equitypartners.com.au

EUROPE Ltd.
Mihalyi Judit
Budapest
Beg utca 3-5.
HU-1022
Hungary
36-1-326-8256
judit@europe-ltd.com

Managing Partner Timothy Bernardez
Evergreen Pacific Partners
1700 Seventh Avenue
Suite 2300
Seattle, Washington 98101
206-262-4709
tbernardez@eppcapital.com

Managing Partner Thomas McGill
Evergreen Pacific Partners
1700 Seventh Avenue

VENTURE CAPITAL DIRECTORY

Suite 2300
Seattle, Washington 98101
206-262-4709
tjmcgill@eppcapital.com

Managing Partner Michael Nibarger
Evergreen Pacific Partners
1700 Seventh Avenue
Suite 2300
Seattle, Washington 98101
206-262-4709
mnibarger@eppcapital.com

CFO Timothy Brillon
Evergreen Pacific Partners
1700 Seventh Avenue
Suite 2300
Seattle, Washington 98101
206-262-4709
tbrillon@eppcapital.com

Hong Kong

Units 1208-1209, Level 12, Core F, Cyberport 3100 Cyberport Road
Excelsior Capital Asia
 LawrenceGary
852-2230-9800
gary.lawrence@excelcapasia.com

Hong Kong

Units 1208-1209, Level 12, Core F, Cyberport 3100 Cyberport Road
Excelsior Capital Asia
 KentMichael
852-2230-9800
michael.kent@excelcapasia.com

Hong Kong

Units 1208-1209, Level 12, Core F, Cyberport 3100 Cyberport Road
Excelsior Capital Asia
 ThavikBordin
852-2230-9800
bordin.thavik@excelcapasia.com

VENTURE CAPITAL DIRECTORY

Hong Kong

Units 1208-1209, Level 12, Core F, Cyberport 3100 Cyberport Road
Excelsior Capital Asia
 YungKimberley
852-2230-9800
kimberley.yung@excelcapasia.com

Hong Kong

Units 1208-1209, Level 12, Core F, Cyberport 3100 Cyberport Road
Excelsior Capital Asia
 FrickThomas
852-2230-9800
thomas.frick@excelcapasia.com

Hong Kong

Units 1208-1209, Level 12, Core F, Cyberport 3100 Cyberport Road
Excelsior Capital Asia
 YangJohn
852-2230-9800
john.yang@excelcapasia.com

Hong Kong

Units 1208-1209, Level 12, Core F, Cyberport 3100 Cyberport Road
Excelsior Capital Asia
 TaLynn
852-2230-9800
lynn.ta@excelcapasia.com

Hong Kong

Units 1208-1209, Level 12, Core F, Cyberport 3100 Cyberport Road
Excelsior Capital Asia
 ChiuDicken
852-2230-9800
dicken.chiu@excelcapasia.com

Hong Kong

Units 1208-1209, Level 12, Core F, Cyberport 3100 Cyberport Road
Excelsior Capital Asia
 HuangJo
852-2230-9800

VENTURE CAPITAL DIRECTORY

jo.huang@excelcapasia.com

Managing Partner Keith Fox
Exeter Capital Partners
1 Liberty Square
Suite 1200
Boston, Massachusetts 2109
617-224-0100
keith.fox@exeterfunds.com

Partner Richard Campin
Exponent Private Equity LLP
12 Henrietta Street
London
WC2E 8LH
United Kingdom
44-20-7845-8520
richard.campin@exponentpe.com

Partner Chris Graham
Exponent Private Equity LLP
12 Henrietta Street
London
WC2E 8LH
United Kingdom
44-20-7845-8520
chris.graham@exponentpe.com

Partner Hugh Richards
Exponent Private Equity LLP
12 Henrietta Street
London
WC2E 8LH
United Kingdom
44-20-7845-8520
hugh.richards@exponentpe.com

Partner Tom Sweet-Escott
Exponent Private Equity LLP
12 Henrietta Street
London
WC2E 8LH
United Kingdom
44-20-7845-8520
tom.sweetescott@exponentpe.com

VENTURE CAPITAL DIRECTORY

Director Simon Baines
Exponent Private Equity LLP
12 Henrietta Street
London
WC2E 8LH
United Kingdom
44-20-7845-8520
simon.baines@exponentpe.com

Director Jack Edmondson
Exponent Private Equity LLP
12 Henrietta Street
London
WC2E 8LH
United Kingdom
44-20-7845-8520
jack.edmondson@exponentpe.com

Director Richard Lenane
Exponent Private Equity LLP
12 Henrietta Street
London
WC2E 8LH
United Kingdom
44-20-7845-8520
richard.lenane@exponentpe.com

Finance Director Craig Vickery
Exponent Private Equity LLP
12 Henrietta Street
London
WC2E 8LH
United Kingdom
44-20-7845-8520
craig.vickery@exponentpe.com

Chairman and CEO David Moross
Falconhead Capital LLC
450 Park Avenue
3rd Floor
New York, New York 10022
212-634-3304

General Partner David Gubbay
Falconhead Capital LLC
450 Park Avenue

VENTURE CAPITAL DIRECTORY

3rd Floor
New York, New York 10022
212-634-3304
davegubbay@falconheadcapital.com

General Partner Brian Crosby
Falconhead Capital LLC
450 Park Avenue
3rd Floor
New York, New York 10022
212-634-3304
bcrosby@falconheadcapital.com

General Partner Zuher Ladak
Falconhead Capital LLC
450 Park Avenue
3rd Floor
New York, New York 10022
212-634-3304

Vice President Jason Turowsky
Falconhead Capital LLC
450 Park Avenue
3rd Floor
New York, New York 10022
212-634-3304

Associate Edward Wong
Falconhead Capital LLC
450 Park Avenue
3rd Floor
New York, New York 10022
212-634-3304

General Counsel Lisa Anastos
Falconhead Capital LLC
450 Park Avenue
3rd Floor
New York, New York 10022
212-634-3304

VENTURE CAPITAL DIRECTORY

CFO Glen Bushery
Falconhead Capital LLC
450 Park Avenue
3rd Floor
New York, New York 10022
212-634-3304

China
 200021
ShanghaiSuite 1502-03, One Corporate Avenue
222 Hubin Road, Luwan District
Fidelity Asia Ventures
 TamBenson
81-21-6386-8622

China
 200021
ShanghaiSuite 1502-03, One Corporate Avenue
222 Hubin Road, Luwan District
Fidelity Asia Ventures
 QianYu
81-21-6386-8622

Hong Kong

17/F One International Finance Centre1 Harbour View Street, Central
Fidelity Asia Ventures
 AuerbachDaniel
852-2629-2800

Hong Kong

17/F One International Finance Centre1 Harbour View Street, Central
Fidelity Asia Ventures
 ChenNorman
852-2629-2800

Hong Kong

17/F One International Finance Centre1 Harbour View Street, Central
Fidelity Asia Ventures
 ChuaTed
852-2629-2800

Hong Kong

VENTURE CAPITAL DIRECTORY

17/F One International Finance Centre1 Harbour View Street, Central
Fidelity Asia Ventures
 ChengAlbert
852-2629-2800

Partner Nick Martin
Fidelity Equity Partners
25 Cannon Street
London
EC4M 5TA
United Kingdom
44-20-7664-2303
nick.martin@fidelity.com

Managing Partner Rob Ketterson
Fidelity Equity Partners
One Federal Street
27th Floor
Boston, Massachusetts 2110
617-392-2448
rob.ketterson@fidelityep.com

Partner Brooke Ablon
Fidelity Equity Partners
One Federal Street
27th Floor
Boston, Massachusetts 2110
617-392-2448
brooke.ablon@fidelity.com

Senior Associate David Nemeskal
Fidelity Equity Partners
One Federal Street
27th Floor
Boston, Massachusetts 2110
617-392-2448
david.nemeskal@fidelity.com

Associate Evan McCormick
Fidelity Equity Partners
One Federal Street
27th Floor
Boston, Massachusetts 2110
617-392-2448
evan.mcCormick@fidelity.com

VENTURE CAPITAL DIRECTORY

Associate Michael York
Fidelity Equity Partners
One Federal Street
27th Floor
Boston, Massachusetts 2110
617-392-2448
michael.york@fidelity.com

Investment Director Peter Wright
Finance Wales Investments Ltd.
Oakleigh House
Park Place
Cardiff
CF10 3DQ
United Kingdom
44-29-2033-8100
peter.wright@financewales.co.uk

Risk Director Mike Davies
Finance Wales Investments Ltd.
Oakleigh House
Park Place
Cardiff
CF10 3DQ
United Kingdom
44-29-2033-8100
mike.davies@financewales.co.uk

firstVentury Equity GmbH
Managing Partner
George M. Rehm
Seedammstrasse 3
CH-8808 Pfäffikon
Switzerland
49-6221-43854-0
grehm@firstventury.com

firstVentury Equity GmbH
Partner
Niall P. Davis
Seedammstrasse 3
CH-8808 Pfäffikon
Switzerland
49-6221-43854-0
ndavis@firstventury.com

VENTURE CAPITAL DIRECTORY

firstVentury Equity GmbH
Managing Partner
David Hartford
Seedammstrasse 3
CH-8808 Pfäffikon
Switzerland
49-6221-43854-0
dhartford@firstventury.com

firstVentury Equity GmbH
Managing Partner
Uwe R. Feuersenger
Seedammstrasse 3
CH-8808 Pfäffikon
Switzerland
49-6221-43854-0
ufeuersenger@firstventury.com

firstVentury Equity GmbH
Partner
Frank Mühlenbeck
Seedammstrasse 3
CH-8808 Pfäffikon
Switzerland
49-6221-43854-0
fmuehlenbeck@firstventury.com

firstVentury Equity GmbH
Managing Partner
Michael W. Kelly
Seedammstrasse 3
CH-8808 Pfäffikon
Switzerland
49-6221-43854-0
mkelly@firstventury.com

Shai Beilis
Formula Ventures Ltd.
11 Galgalei Haplada
P.O.Box 2062
Herzliya 46120
Israel
972-9-960-1800
shai@formulaventures.com

Nir Linchevski

VENTURE CAPITAL DIRECTORY

Formula Ventures Ltd.
11 Galgalei Haplada
P.O.Box 2062
Herzliya 46120
Israel
972-9-960-1800
nir@formulaventures.com

Benny Maidan
Formula Ventures Ltd.
11 Galgalei Haplada
P.O.Box 2062
Herzliya 46120
Israel
972-9-960-1800
maidanb@formula.co.il

Ran Mokady
Formula Ventures Ltd.
11 Galgalei Haplada
P.O.Box 2062
Herzliya 46120
Israel
972-9-960-1800
ran@formulaventures.com

Varda Sagiv
Formula Ventures Ltd.
11 Galgalei Haplada
P.O.Box 2062
Herzliya 46120
Israel
972-9-960-1800
varda@formulaventures.com

Ariel Sella
Formula Ventures Ltd.
11 Galgalei Haplada
P.O.Box 2062
Herzliya 46120
Israel
972-9-960-1800

General Partner Bradford Freeman
Freeman Spogli & Co.
11100 Santa Monica Boulevard

VENTURE CAPITAL DIRECTORY

Suite 1900
Los Angeles, California 90025
310-444-1822

General Partner Mark Doran
Freeman Spogli & Co.
299 Park Avenue
20th Floor
New York, New York 10171
212-758-2555

General Partner Todd Halloran
Freeman Spogli & Co.
299 Park Avenue
20th Floor
New York, New York 10171
212-758-2555

General Partner Jon Ralph
Freeman Spogli & Co.
11100 Santa Monica Boulevard
Suite 1900
Los Angeles, California 90025
310-444-1822
jralph@freemanspogli.com

General Partner John Roth
Freeman Spogli & Co.
299 Park Avenue
20th Floor
New York, New York 10171
212-758-2555

General Partner J. Frederick Simmons
Freeman Spogli & Co.
11100 Santa Monica Boulevard
Suite 1900
Los Angeles, California 90025
310-444-1822
fsimmons@freemanspogli.com

General Partner William Wardlaw
Freeman Spogli & Co.
11100 Santa Monica Boulevard
Suite 1900
Los Angeles, California 90025

VENTURE CAPITAL DIRECTORY

310-444-1822
bwardlaw@freemanspogli.com

Brad Brutocao
Freeman Spogli & Co.
11100 Santa Monica Boulevard
Suite 1900
Los Angeles, California 90025
310-444-1822
bbrutocao@freemanspogli.com

Benjamin Geiger
Freeman Spogli & Co.
11100 Santa Monica Boulevard
Suite 1900
Los Angeles, California 90025
310-444-1822

John Hwang
Freeman Spogli & Co.
11100 Santa Monica Boulevard
Suite 1900
Los Angeles, California 90025
310-444-1822
jhwang@freemanspogli.com

Christian Johnson
Freeman Spogli & Co.
11100 Santa Monica Boulevard
Suite 1900
Los Angeles, California 90025
310-444-1822

Trevor Parris
Freeman Spogli & Co.
11100 Santa Monica Boulevard
Suite 1900
Los Angeles, California 90025
310-444-1822
tparris@freemanspogli.com

Managing Director Charles Kireker
Freshtracks Capital
5 Park Street
P.O. Box 927
Middlebury, Vermont 5753

VENTURE CAPITAL DIRECTORY

802-388-6283
charlie@freshtrackscap.com

Managing Director Cairn Cross
Freshtracks Capital
5 Park Street
P.O. Box 927
Middlebury, Vermont 5753
802-388-6283
cairn@freshtrackscap.com

Managing Director Timothy Davis
Freshtracks Capital
5 Park Street
P.O. Box 927
Middlebury, Vermont 5753
802-388-6283

Associate Lee Bouyea
Freshtracks Capital
5 Park Street
P.O. Box 927
Middlebury, Vermont 5753
802-388-6283

Chairman and Managing Director Rodney Goldstein
Frontenac Company
135 South La Salle Street
Suite 3800
Chicago, Illinois 60603
312-368-0044
rgoldstein@frontenac.com

Managing Director Patrick Blandford
Frontenac Company
135 South La Salle Street
Suite 3800
Chicago, Illinois 60603
312-368-0044
pblandford@frontenac.com

Managing Director Paul Carbery
Frontenac Company
135 South La Salle Street
Suite 3800
Chicago, Illinois 60603

VENTURE CAPITAL DIRECTORY

312-368-0044
pcarbery@frontenac.com

Managing Director James Cowie
Frontenac Company
135 South La Salle Street
Suite 3800
Chicago, Illinois 60603
312-368-0044
jcowie@frontenac.com

Managing Director Walter Florence
Frontenac Company
135 South La Salle Street
Suite 3800
Chicago, Illinois 60603
312-368-0044
wflorence@frontenac.com

Managing Director Troy Noard
Frontenac Company
135 South La Salle Street
Suite 3800
Chicago, Illinois 60603
312-368-0044
tnoard@frontenac.com

Managing Director Jeremy Silverman
Frontenac Company
135 South La Salle Street
Suite 3800
Chicago, Illinois 60603
312-368-0044
jsilverman@frontenac.com

Vice President Andrew Seger
Frontenac Company
135 South La Salle Street
Suite 3800
Chicago, Illinois 60603
312-368-0044
aseger@frontenac.com

Associate George Maglares
Frontenac Company
135 South La Salle Street

VENTURE CAPITAL DIRECTORY

Suite 3800
Chicago, Illinois 60603
312-368-0044
gmaglares@frontenac.com

Associate Chad Feingold
Frontenac Company
135 South La Salle Street
Suite 3800
Chicago, Illinois 60603
312-368-0044
cfeingold@frontenac.com

Vice President Ronald Kuehl
Frontenac Company
135 South La Salle Street
Suite 3800
Chicago, Illinois 60603
312-368-0044
rkuehl@frontenac.com

Associate Parker Davis
Frontenac Company
135 South La Salle Street
Suite 3800
Chicago, Illinois 60603
312-368-0044
pdavis@frontenac.com

Founder Partner and Principal Kabra Atim
Frontline Venture Services Pvt Ltd.,
515 "Midas" Sahar Plaza,
Andheri-Kurla Road, Andheri (E),
Mumbai - 400 059,
India
91-22-2826-4534
atim@frontlinestrategy.com

Managing Partner Joël Flichy
Galileo Partners
106 rue de l'Université
FR-75007 Paris
France
33-1-5359-4500
jflichy@galileo.fr

VENTURE CAPITAL DIRECTORY

Partner Christophe Viet
Galileo Partners
106 rue de l'Université
FR-75007 Paris
France
33-1-5359-4500
cviet@galileo.fr

Partner Jean-Michel Guichot
Galileo Partners
106 rue de l'Université
FR-75007 Paris
France
33-1-5359-4500
jmguichot@galileo.fr

Partner Régis Saleur
Galileo Partners
106 rue de l'Université
FR-75007 Paris
France
33-1-5359-4500
rsaleur@galileo.fr

Partner François Duliège
Galileo Partners
106 rue de l'Université
FR-75007 Paris
France
33-1-5359-4500

Co-Founder and Managing Director Louis Desmarais
Garage Technology Ventures Canada
1501 McGill College Ave.
Suite 2240
Montreal Quebec H3A 3M8
Canada
514-878-1400
desmarais@garagecanada.com

Co-Founder and Managing Director Tom Sweeney
Garage Technology Ventures Canada
1501 McGill College Ave.
Suite 2240
Montreal Quebec H3A 3M8
Canada

VENTURE CAPITAL DIRECTORY

514-878-1400
sweeney@garagecanada.com

Hong Kong

Suite 3601, Cheung Kong Center2 Queen's Road Central
GEMS Ltd.
 MurraySimon
852-2838-0093

Hong Kong

Suite 3601, Cheung Kong Center2 Queen's Road Central
GEMS Ltd.
 SpenderGeoff
852-2838-0093

Hong Kong

Suite 3601, Cheung Kong Center2 Queen's Road Central
GEMS Ltd.
 LeongWinston
852-2838-0093
wleong@gems.com.hk

Hong Kong

Suite 3601, Cheung Kong Center2 Queen's Road Central
GEMS Ltd.
 Van OppenDavid
852-2838-0093
vanoppen@gems.com.hk

Hong Kong

Suite 3601, Cheung Kong Center2 Queen's Road Central
GEMS Ltd.
 SoutarGraham
852-2838-0093
gsoutar@gems.com.hk

Hong Kong

Suite 3601, Cheung Kong Center2 Queen's Road Central
GEMS Ltd.
 PowellNick

VENTURE CAPITAL DIRECTORY

852-2838-0093

Hong Kong

Suite 3601, Cheung Kong Center2 Queen's Road Central
GEMS Ltd.
 WilmerFergus
852-2838-0093

Managing Director Florian Wendelstadt
General Atlantic LLC
83 Pall Mall, Sixth Floor
London
SW1Y 5ES
United Kingdom
44-20-7484-3200
fwendelstadt@generalatlantic.com

Chairman Steven Denning
General Atlantic LLC
Three Pickwick Plaza
Greenwich, Connecticut 6830
203-629-8600
sdenning@generalatlantic.com

CEO William Ford
General Atlantic LLC
Three Pickwick Plaza
Greenwich, Connecticut 6830
203-629-8600
wford@generalatlantic.com

Managing Director William Grabe
General Atlantic LLC
Three Pickwick Plaza
Greenwich, Connecticut 6830
203-629-8600
wgrabe@generalatlantic.com

Managing Director David Hodgson
General Atlantic LLC
Three Pickwick Plaza
Greenwich, Connecticut 6830
203-629-8600
dhodgson@generalatlantic.com

VENTURE CAPITAL DIRECTORY

Managing Director Mark Dzialga
General Atlantic LLC
Three Pickwick Plaza
Greenwich, Connecticut 6830
203-629-8600
mdzialga@generalatlantic.com

Managing Director Peter Bloom
General Atlantic LLC
Three Pickwick Plaza
Greenwich, Connecticut 6830
203-629-8600
pbloom@generalatlantic.com

Managing Director Rene Kern
General Atlantic LLC
Three Pickwick Plaza
Greenwich, Connecticut 6830
203-629-8600
rkern@generalatlantic.com

Managing Director Matthew Nimetz
General Atlantic LLC
Three Pickwick Plaza
Greenwich, Connecticut 6830
203-629-8600
mnimetz@generalatlantic.com

Managing Director Franchon Smithson
General Atlantic LLC
Three Pickwick Plaza
Greenwich, Connecticut 6830
203-629-8600
fsmithson@generalatlantic.com

Managing Director Tom Tinsley
General Atlantic LLC
2401 Pennsylvania Ave. N.W.
Suite 480
Washington, District of Columbia 20037
202-263-5820
ttinsley@generalatlantic.com

Managing Director Ray Bingham
General Atlantic LLC
228 Hamilton Avenue

VENTURE CAPITAL DIRECTORY

Palo Alto, California 94301
650-251-7800
rbingham@generalatlantic.com

Managing Director Marc McMorris
General Atlantic LLC
228 Hamilton Avenue
Palo Alto, California 94301
650-251-7800
mmcmorris@generalatlantic.com

Managing Director Anton Levy
General Atlantic LLC
Three Pickwick Plaza
Greenwich, Connecticut 6830
203-629-8600
alevy@generalatlantic.com

Managing Partner John Hawkins
Generation Partners
One Maritime Plaza
Suite 1425
San Francisco, California 94111
415-646-8620
hawkins@generation.com

Managing Partner Mark Jennings
Generation Partners
One Greenwich Office Park
Greenwich, Connecticut 6831
203-422-8200
jennings@generation.com

Partner Peter Campbell
Generation Partners
One Greenwich Office Park
Greenwich, Connecticut 6831
203-422-8200
campbell@generation.com

Partner Andrew Hertzmark
Generation Partners
One Greenwich Office Park
Greenwich, Connecticut 6831
203-422-8200
hertzmark@generation.com

VENTURE CAPITAL DIRECTORY

Vice President Louis Marino
Generation Partners
One Greenwich Office Park
Greenwich, Connecticut 6831
203-422-8200
marino@generation.com

Controller Dorothy Jatzen
Generation Partners
One Greenwich Office Park
Greenwich, Connecticut 6831
203-422-8200
jatzen@generation.com

Founding Partner Paul Hobby
Genesis Park LP
2131 San Felipe
Houston, Texas 77019
713-521-1980
phobby@genesis-park.com

Founding Partner Neil Kelley
Genesis Park LP
2131 San Felipe
Houston, Texas 77019
713-521-1980

Founding Partner Peter Shaper
Genesis Park LP
2131 San Felipe
Houston, Texas 77019
713-521-1980

Founding Partner Steven Gibson
Genesis Park LP
2131 San Felipe
Houston, Texas 77019
713-521-1980

CFO Bonnie Lewis
Genesis Park LP
2131 San Felipe
Houston, Texas 77019
713-521-1980
blewis@genesis-park.com

VENTURE CAPITAL DIRECTORY

President Thomas Arland
GF Private Equity Group, LLC
135 Burnett Drive
Suite 101
Durango, Colorado 81301
970-764-6300

Vice President David Fallace
GF Private Equity Group, LLC
135 Burnett Drive
Suite 101
Durango, Colorado 81301
970-764-6300

Vice President Mahesh Vaidya
GF Private Equity Group, LLC
135 Burnett Drive
Suite 101
Durango, Colorado 81301
970-764-6300

Vice President Ken Lucas
GF Private Equity Group, LLC
135 Burnett Drive
Suite 101
Durango, Colorado 81301
970-764-6300

Vice President James Thompson
GF Private Equity Group, LLC
135 Burnett Drive
Suite 101
Durango, Colorado 81301
970-764-6300

Vice President Chris Metcalf
GF Private Equity Group, LLC
135 Burnett Drive
Suite 101
Durango, Colorado 81301
970-764-6300

Managing Director Mark Tagliaferri
GI Partners
5th Floor
35 Portman Square

VENTURE CAPITAL DIRECTORY

London
W1H 6LR
United Kingdom
44-20-7034-1120
mark@gipartners.co.uk

Managing Director Phil Kaziewicz
GI Partners
5th Floor
35 Portman Square
London
W1H 6LR
United Kingdom
44-20-7034-1120
phil@gipartners.co.uk

Managing Director Al Foglio
GI Partners
5th Floor
35 Portman Square
London
W1H 6LR
United Kingdom
44-20-7034-1120
al@gipartners.co.uk

Managing Director Brad Altberger
GI Partners
5th Floor
35 Portman Square
London
W1H 6LR
United Kingdom
44-20-7034-1120
brad@gipartners.co.uk

Executive Managing Director Rick Magnuson
GI Partners
2180 Sand Hill Road
Suite 210
Menlo Park, California 94025
650-233-3600
rick@gipartners.com

VENTURE CAPITAL DIRECTORY

Managing Director Eric Harrison
GI Partners
2180 Sand Hill Road
Suite 210
Menlo Park, California 94025
650-233-3600
eric@gipartners.com

Managing Director Howard Park
GI Partners
2180 Sand Hill Road
Suite 210
Menlo Park, California 94025
650-233-3600
howard@gipartners.com

Managing Director Andrew Tainiter
GI Partners
2180 Sand Hill Road
Suite 210
Menlo Park, California 94025
650-233-3600
andrew@gipartners.com

Director Alexander Fraser
GI Partners
2180 Sand Hill Road
Suite 210
Menlo Park, California 94025
650-233-3600
alexander@gipartners.com

Senior Associate David Mace
GI Partners
2180 Sand Hill Road
Suite 210
Menlo Park, California 94025
650-233-3600
david@gipartners.com

Associate Jeff Sheu
GI Partners
2180 Sand Hill Road
Suite 210
Menlo Park, California 94025
650-233-3600

VENTURE CAPITAL DIRECTORY

jeff@gipartners.com

Associate Kevin English
GI Partners
2180 Sand Hill Road
Suite 210
Menlo Park, California 94025
650-233-3600
kevin@gipartners.com

Managing Director Jonathan Bloch
GKM Ventures
11150 Santa Monica Boulevard
Suite 825
Los Angeles, California 90025
310-268-2637
jbloch@gkmventures.com

Managing Director Emanuel Gerard
GKM Ventures
11150 Santa Monica Boulevard
Suite 825
Los Angeles, California 90025
310-268-2637

Managing Director John Morris
GKM Ventures
11150 Santa Monica Boulevard
Suite 825
Los Angeles, California 90025
310-268-2637
jmorris@gkmventures.com

Managing Director David Stastny
GKM Ventures
11150 Santa Monica Boulevard
Suite 825
Los Angeles, California 90025
310-268-2637
dstastny@gkmventures.com

Venture Partner Ravi Chiruvolu
GKM Ventures
11150 Santa Monica Boulevard
Suite 825
Los Angeles, California 90025

VENTURE CAPITAL DIRECTORY

310-268-2637
rchiruvolu@gkmventures.com

Venture Partner Ralph Eschenbach
GKM Ventures
11150 Santa Monica Boulevard
Suite 825
Los Angeles, California 90025
310-268-2637
reschenbach@gkmventures.com

Chairman and Managing Director David Evans
Glencoe Capital, LLC
222 West Adams Street
Suite 1000
Chicago, Illinois 60606
312-795-6300
devans@glencap.com
Vice Chairman and Managing Director William McGrath
Glencoe Capital, LLC
222 West Adams Street
Suite 1000
Chicago, Illinois 60606
312-795-6300
wmcgrath@glencap.com

Principal and Director of Portfolio Management Louis Manetti
Glencoe Capital, LLC
222 West Adams Street
Suite 1000
Chicago, Illinois 60606
312-795-6300

Principal G. Douglas Patterson
Glencoe Capital, LLC
222 West Adams Street
Suite 1000
Chicago, Illinois 60606
312-795-6300

Principal Jason Duzan
Glencoe Capital, LLC
222 West Adams Street
Suite 1000
Chicago, Illinois 60606
312-795-6300

VENTURE CAPITAL DIRECTORY

jduzan@glencap.com

CFO and COO Beth Satterfield
Glencoe Capital, LLC
222 West Adams Street
Suite 1000
Chicago, Illinois 60606
312-795-6300

Vice President Benjamin Kahn
Glencoe Capital, LLC
222 West Adams Street
Suite 1000
Chicago, Illinois 60606
312-795-6300

Vice President Rocky Golem
Glencoe Capital, LLC
222 West Adams Street
Suite 1000
Chicago, Illinois 60606
312-795-6300
bkahn@glencap.com

Vice President Eric O'Dell
Glencoe Capital, LLC
222 West Adams Street
Suite 1000
Chicago, Illinois 60606
312-795-6300

Associate Joshua Becker
Glencoe Capital, LLC
222 West Adams Street
Suite 1000
Chicago, Illinois 60606
312-795-6300

Analyst Carrie Matusiak
Glencoe Capital, LLC
222 West Adams Street
Suite 1000
Chicago, Illinois 60606
312-795-6300

Global Equity Partners Beteiligungs-Management AG

VENTURE CAPITAL DIRECTORY

Managing Director
Michael Tojner
Mariahilfer Strasse 19-21
AT-1060 Vienna
Austria
43-1-581-8390
m.tojner@gep.at

Global Equity Partners Beteiligungs-Management AG
Senior Partner
Wilhelm R. Tschol
Mariahilfer Strasse 19-21
AT-1060 Vienna
Austria
43-1-581-8390
w.tschol@gep.at

Global Equity Partners Beteiligungs-Management AG
Managing Director
Herbert Herdlicka
Mariahilfer Strasse 19-21
AT-1060 Vienna
Austria
43-1-581-8390
h.herdlicka@gep.at

Global Equity Partners Beteiligungs-Management AG
Investment Analyst
Erik Feichtinger
Mariahilfer Strasse 19-21
AT-1060 Vienna
Austria
43-1-581-8390
e.feichtinger@gep.at

Global Equity Partners Beteiligungs-Management AG
Senior Partner
William Rees
Mariahilfer Strasse 19-21
AT-1060 Vienna
Austria
43-1-581-8390
w.rees@gep.at

Global Finance S.A.
Managing Partner Angelos Plakopitas

VENTURE CAPITAL DIRECTORY

14 Filikis Eterias Square
GR-10673 Athens
Greece
30-210-720-8900

Global Finance S.A.
Partner Theodore Kiakidis
14 Filikis Eterias Square
GR-10673 Athens
Greece
30-210-720-8900
kiakidis@globalfinance.gr

Japan
102-0084
Tokyo5F Sumitomo Fudosan Kojimachi Bldg
5-1 Nibancho, Chiyoda-ku
Globis Capital Partners & Co.
HoriYoshito
81-3-5272-3939
yhori@globis.co.jp

Japan
102-0084
Tokyo5F Sumitomo Fudosan Kojimachi Bldg
5-1 Nibancho, Chiyoda-ku
Globis Capital Partners & Co.
KariyazonoSoichi
81-3-5272-3939

Japan
102-0084
Tokyo5F Sumitomo Fudosan Kojimachi Bldg
5-1 Nibancho, Chiyoda-ku
Globis Capital Partners & Co.
KobayashiMasashi
81-3-5272-3939

Japan
102-0084
Tokyo5F Sumitomo Fudosan Kojimachi Bldg
5-1 Nibancho, Chiyoda-ku
Globis Capital Partners & Co.
InoueKen
81-3-5272-3939

VENTURE CAPITAL DIRECTORY

Japan
102-0084
Tokyo5F Sumitomo Fudosan Kojimachi Bldg
5-1 Nibancho, Chiyoda-ku
Globis Capital Partners & Co.
InoueTakuo
81-3-5272-3939

Japan
102-0084
Tokyo5F Sumitomo Fudosan Kojimachi Bldg
5-1 Nibancho, Chiyoda-ku
Globis Capital Partners & Co.
HataTakaaki
81-3-5272-3939

GMT Communications Partners III LLP
Sackville House
40 Piccadilly
London
W1J 0DR
United Kingdom
44-20-7292-9333
massimo.prelz@gmtpartners.com

Managing Director David Dominik
Golden Gate Capital
One Embarcadero Center
33rd Floor
San Francisco, California 94111
415-627-4500
ddominik@goldengatecap.com

Principal John Knoll
Golden Gate Capital
One Embarcadero Center
33rd Floor
San Francisco, California 94111
415-627-4500
jknoll@goldengatecap.com

President Lawrence Golub
Golub Capital
551 Madison Avenue
New York, New York 10022
212-750-6060

VENTURE CAPITAL DIRECTORY

lgolub@golubcapital.com

Managing Director Edward Grace III
Grace Venture Partners, L.P.
SunTrust Center, Suite 1850
200 South Orange Avenue
Orlando, Florida 32801
407-835-7900
ngrace@graceventure.com

Managing Partner Gregory Belmont
Grand Central Holdings, LLC
575 Lexington Avenue #2840
New York, New York 10022
212-625-9710
belmont@grandcentralholdings.com

Managing Partner Wendell Reilly
Grapevine Partners LLC
400 Colony Square
Suite 200
Atlanta, Georgia 30361
404-870-9106
wreilly@grapevinepartners.com

Grazia Equity GmbH
Managing Director Alec Rauschenbusch
Breitscheidstrasse 10
DE-70174 Stuttgart
Germany
49-711-907109-0

Managing Partner Christopher Gaffney
Great Hill Partners, LLC
One Liberty Square
Boston, Massachusetts 2109
617-790-9400
cgaffney@greathillpartners.com

Managing Partner Dave Gross
Great Pacific Capital LLC
610 Anacapa Street
Santa Barbara, California 93101
805-966-1000
dave.gross@greatpacificcapital.com

VENTURE CAPITAL DIRECTORY

Greenfield Capital Partners BV
Managing Partner Paul Janssens
Huizerstraatweg 111
NL-1411 GM Naarden
Netherlands
31-35-699-3900
janssens@greenfield.nl

Greenfield Capital Partners BV
Investment Manager Roel Harting
Huizerstraatweg 111
NL-1411 GM Naarden
Netherlands
31-35-699-3900
harting@greenfield.nl

Managing Director Steve Brotman
Greenhill SAVP
300 Park Avenue
New York, New York 10022
212-389-1600
sbrotman@greenhill.com

Managing General Partner Frank Adams
Grotech Capital Group
9690 Deereco Road
Suite 800
Timonium, Maryland 21093
410-560-2000
fadams@grotech.com

Founder and Managing Partner Michael Edell
GroundWork Equity, LLC
826 Calle Plano
Camarillo, California 93012
805-383-6288 ext. 101
medell@groundworkequity.com

President and CEO David Levi
GrowthWorks Capital Ltd.
Box 11170, Royal Centre
2600 - 1055 West Georgia Street
Vancouver British Columbia V6E 3R5
Canada
604-633-1418
david.levi@growthworks.ca

www.ingramcontent.com/pod-product-compliance
Lightning Source LLC
Chambersburg PA
CBHW081428220526
45466CB00008B/2301